W9-AOZ-956

3   0570 00567980 2

This book is for Dorothy Sumner

First published 1983 by Laura Ashley Limited, Carno, Powys, Wales
© City of Manchester Cultural Services 1983

ISBN O 9508913 0 4

Produced by ♂P Studio Press Print Group 021-359 3151   Printed in England

Fabric of Society

A Century of People and their Clothes 1770-1870

Essays inspired by the collections at
Platt Hall, The Gallery of English Costume, Manchester

By Jane Tozer and Sarah Levitt
Photographs by Mark Cobley
with a Foreword by Laura Ashley

Foreword

I first stepped over the threshold of Platt Hall two years ago and the hours
I have spent there since have been a total enchantment to me.
In one of the prettiest buildings in England is housed a collection of costumes
expressing the hopes and dreams, as well the duties and orderliness, of the
town and country people of the region during the 18th and 19th centuries.
The poignancy of the collection is heightened by the fact that the era it
represents coincides with the focus of calico printing on Manchester itself.
Here you will find both the rich silks and embroideries of court dress, and the
no less appealing printed cottons of local manufacture. The farmers' and
mill-owners' wives of Cheshire and Lancashire used these wonderful printed
cottons and chintzes to create exquisite gowns for special occasions, and
simple dresses for morning wear. You can see the respectable day dresses,
millinery and lace of the urban middle classes, together with the aprons,
cloaks and handsome workwear of country women, giving a total picture of a
vanished culture.

Laura Ashley

Contents

Platt Hall

The Platt Estate and the Worsley Family

Major General Charles Worsley (1622-1656) steel engraving by Augustus Fox from an original painting by William Dobson (1610-46).

The Platt Estate dates from the early 12th century, when it was owned by the monastic order of the Knights Hospitaller of St. John of Jerusalem. In 1190 it was given by the order to Richard de la More, whose descendants took the name Platt in the 13th century. Edmund Platt sold the estate to Raphe Worsley in 1625.

The Worsley family, a branch of the Yorkshire family of the Duchess of Kent, claimed descent from Elias de Workesley, Lord of Worsley, who died at Rhodes while on Crusade to the Holy Land. Raphe Worsley's fortune came from the textile trade, supplying the handloom weavers with yarn, and selling the cloth. He was a man of Puritan sympathies and his son Charles Worsley (1622-1656) became one of Cromwell's most trusted officers.

At 28 years of age, in 1650, he had already risen to the rank of Lieutenant-Colonel, and raised a regiment of soldiers in the Manchester area. His career attracted attention and he was given command of Cromwell's own Regiment. On April 20th, 1653 Charles Worsley led the contingent of foot supporting Cromwell at the dissolution of the Long Parliament. Cromwell ordered the removal of the Mace with the legendary command "Take away that bauble!"; the Mace thereafter remained in Worsley's custody until Parliament was recalled.

Charles Worsley, by now a full Colonel, became Manchester's first MP in 1654. This Parliament was short-lived, and for a time the nation was without parliamentary government, being divided into ten districts, each under the control of a Vice-Gerent. In October 1655, Charles Worsley was created Major-General and Vice-Gerent for Lancashire, Cheshire and Staffordshire. He appears to have carried out his duties with true Puritan zeal, suppressing drunkenness and swearing, disarming Papists, ensuring the proper observance of the Lord's day. "We ordered 200 (ale-houses) to be thrown down at Blackburn, and we are catching up all loose and vile persons." (January 1656).

Major General Worsley died at St. James's Palace at the age of 34, in 1656, after being recalled to London. His brief, distinguished career was marked by conscientious devotion to his work. He was given a funeral with due military honours, and buried in Westminster Abbey.

A blue plaque commemorating Charles Worsley is set in the wall of Platt Hall, though this is not the house that he knew. The present house was built in 1762-4 by John Lees, a textile merchant, who had married Deborah Worsley, heiress to the Platt estates, in 1744. John Lees, and his son Thomas by a former marriage, took the name Carrill-Worsley in 1774. More will be said of the house, and of Thomas Worsley, later on.

A coat of arms of the Worsley family.

In 1906 the Platt Estate came on to the market, and part, including the Hall, was sold for development. Fine trees, and an ancient rookery, were to be chopped down; even worse, the house was to be demolished, and its bricks to be used for building houses and shops. A public outcry was inevitable; fortunately the protest was properly organised by a group of local people, notably William Royle, historian of Rusholme. These early environmentalists chose the name "Platt Fields", which they thought would catch public attention; the park has remained Platt Fields ever since. In July 1907, a deputation waited upon the Lord Mayor, requesting that the City Council should negotiate the purchase of the Platt Estate for the use of the public. On May 7th, 1910, the Lord Mayor opened Platt Fields as a perpetual green space for the people of Manchester, and it has become a beloved part of the lives and memories of local people. William Royle, who did so much to save Platt, is honoured by a memorial in the park.

Platt Hall became an Art Gallery in 1925. Structural alterations had already taken place, and some of the lovely 18th century carved fireplaces had been moved to the Worsley's London house. Nevertheless the staircase and dining room had remained largely unspoiled, and formed a fine setting for paintings, eighteenth century furniture and costume from the City Art Gallery and Rutherston collections.

The dissolution of the Long Parliament, April 1653.

During the second world war the works of art were removed to safety, and Platt Hall was requisitioned for other purposes. In 1947 it began its new life as the Gallery of English Costume.

The Eighteenth Century House

In 1744 the heiresss to the Platt estates, Deborah Worsley, married John Lees, textile merchant. The present hall, which after James Wyatt's Heaton Hall is Manchester's finest Georgian building, was built under John Lees' direction. He commissioned a succession of architects to draw up plans. The first was William Jupp (1728-99) in 1760, followed by John Carr of York (1723-1807) in 1761, and finally Timothy Lightoler (fl. 1758-83) in 1762. Lightoler's plans and elevations were accepted.

The designs of all three architects have been preserved, and some of the drawings by Carr and Lightoler are reproduced here. All three of them produced work in the Palladian manner.

John Carr of York was undoubtedly the most accomplished of the three, and his work is justly celebrated. His design for Platt Hall relied for its façade decoration on an elegant arrangement of proportioned wall areas, with an austere Doric portico. However, the internal layout was unsatisfactory; for example, the coach house was in the west wing, with the kitchen and brew-house, while the stables were at the other end of the house. Apparently Lightoler was called in to modify Carr's plans, rather than to create a completely independent design. His solution was to elongate the proportions of the main block, adding a more ornate Ionic portico, with a pedimented surround to the window above, probably in order to counterbalance the less appealing proportions of the new façade. Lightoler clearly knew, and followed, the Renaissance theory of proportion, using the ratios 9:4 and 3:2 for the windows and 9:4 and 2:1 for the main block. However, comparisons between the two elevations demonstrates Carr's superior skill in the harmonious manipulation of proportion.

Little is known of Timothy Lightoler, but he is believed to have been a Lancashire man. He was almost certainly trained as a craftsman carpenter and woodcarver, and before becoming an architect he may have worked as a decorator. In 1761 he toured England making views and plans of country houses for William Guthrie's *Complete History of the English Peerage* (published in 1763), and this seems to have been a turning point in his career. In 1761 both Lightoler and Carr submitted designs for a dining room at Burton Constable in Yorkshire, and Lightoler's were accepted, much as happened at Platt the following year.

An album of interior designs is preserved at Platt Hall, so that we can envisage part of its splendour, though the house has suffered considerable interior alteration. A late Victorian photograph shows a fine fireplace, perhaps from the drawing room, which was removed to the Worsley's London house before the sale of Platt Hall in 1907.

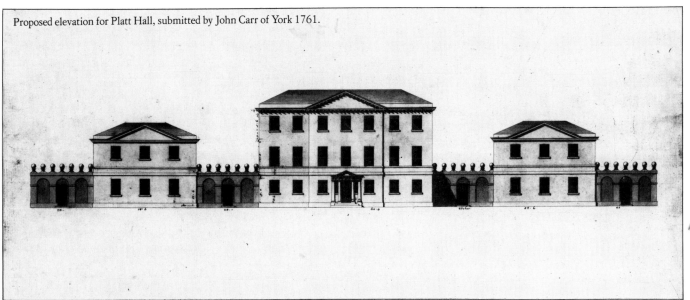

Proposed elevation for Platt Hall, submitted by John Carr of York 1761.

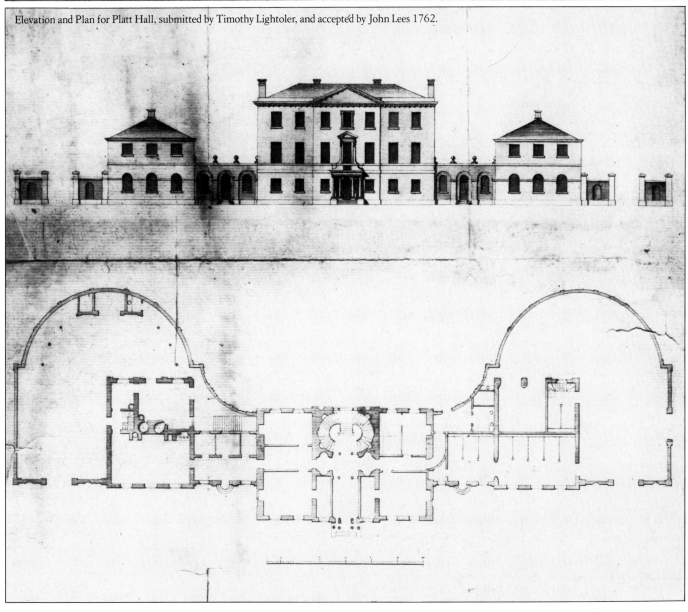

Elevation and Plan for Platt Hall, submitted by Timothy Lightoler, and accepted by John Lees 1762.

Only the delightful dining room, the central room of the first storey, and the staircase with its elegant Venetian window, survive with their original rococo stucco decoration. These areas are undergoing a programme of conservation and restoration. "Paint scrapes" have revealed the successive overpaintings, enabling the colour scheme to be re-created as John and Deborah Lees would have seen it. The oval staircase has recently been repainted in its original subtle colours, stone grey, sand, soft green and blue.

Platt Hall today, in the rose garden of Platt Fields Park, Rusholme, Manchester.

The chief glory of Platt Hall is the dining-room. This would originally have formed the centrepiece of a suite of interconnecting rooms surrounding the staircase, on what Lightoler's plan calls the "Metsonein (sic., for mezzanine) or Parlour Floor". A complete circuit of the rooms began with the common parlour, then the dining room, drawing room and the bed chamber.
The study was perhaps kept apart, and the common parlour would have been for daily use. It was fashionable for English country houses of the mid-eighteenth century to be designed with such a suite, for the better entertainment and admiration of guests. Visitors would pass from room to room to dine, to dance, to play cards, hear music, or take refreshment and ease in the withdrawing room. The furnishings would have been admired and discussed, and the varied decoration enjoyed. Platt Hall's suite of rooms is comparatively modest; nevertheless John Lees must have felt justifiable pride in his dining room. Unfortunately we do not know if he was in the habit of offering lavish entertainment, though there is reason to suspect that he was also modest in this, for he had married into a family of strong dissenting tradition, and he himself was a trustee of Manchester's famous non-conformist chapel at Cross Street.

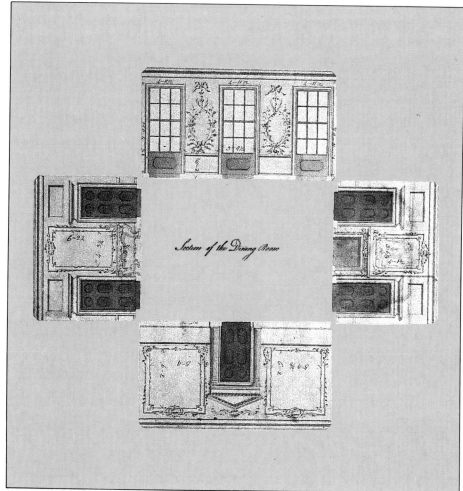

Section of the Dining Room

The re-created colour scheme of the staircase, as John and Deborah Lees might have seen it.

The dining room is still undergoing restoration, a long and complex process. Up to fifteen layers of overpaint are clogging the detail of the stucco and the elaborate carving of the ornate fireplace. What should be a marvel of rococo lightness and delicacy now looks heavy and coarse. Careful stripping of the layers of paint has revealed a colour scheme of soft blue walls, with a slight sandy texture to the plaster. The stucco frames decorating the walls are of stone grey, with highlights picked out in gold leaf. Eventually the successive layers of new paint will be meticulously stripped away, leaving the original colours to be retouched, recreating a room of great elegance.

Interestingly, the same colour combination of blue and grey-white can be found in many 18th century silk dresses, sometimes highlighted with gold and silver thread. One can imagine how the colours of paint and silk would have been enlivened by the flickering of candles and firelight. The texture of the plaster must have added to this effect of subtly stirring light. Modern paints are dull and uniform by comparison.

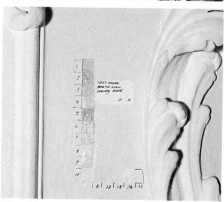

Up to fifteen layers of overpaint cover the original colours.

A detail of *A Summer Evening*
(On the Arno) 1764 oil on canvas
by Richard Wilson (1713-1782)
Commissioned by John Lees to
hang in the dining room of Platt Hall.

Letter from Richard Wilson to James Massey
London Decr 18. 1764

Dear Sir,
        This Day the Landskip was very carefully
packt up and sent according to your order
directed to Your friend Mr Lees — The Picture
represents a Sumer Evening, and is Esteemed by
the first painters here to be my very best
performance, and have kept a Drawing of it in
order to do another for our next exhibition — The
Case packing and Carriage to the Inn comes to
12.^s which twenty five Guineas makes
£26 = 17 = 0.

The receipt of Which I leave to my good friend
Mr Massey, returning you my hearty thanks for
y.^r kind remembrance of

                Dear Sir
                    Y.^r Most Obliged
                        Affectionate Servt
                            R. Wilson.

The Complemt.^s usual
to the Season attend.

                            Decr 28. 1764

Rec.^d of John Lees Esqr twenty six pounds ten shil:
:lings for the Use of M.^r R Wilson

                James Massey

Over the fireplace is fixed a fine landscape by the first great British landscape painter, Richard Wilson (1713-82). The painting was recently exhibited in the Tate Gallery exhibition of Wilson's work, and it is an example of his art at its best. The traditional name of the painting is *River View (On the Arno)*, but Wilson himself called it *A Summer Evening*.

The charming and timeless Italianate landscape is almost certainly imaginary, painted some time after Wilson made his visit to Italy. He would have taken his inspiration from his portfolio of Italian studies.

The painting was commissioned for Platt Hall by John Lees, using James Massey, a mutual acquaintance of Lees and Wilson, as intermediary. Wilson's original letter to Massey survives, requesting payment of 25 guineas for the work and 12 shillings for packing and carriage. John Lees received the painting at Christmas-time, in 1764.

A View of Platt, near Manchester, the seat of John Carill Worsley Esq. signed W. Green. Watercolour by William Green (1760-1823). The costume of the figures is in the fashion of the late 1770s.

A Summer Evening was removed from Platt Hall before the sale to the Corporation in 1907. In 1969 it was purchased from Mrs. Clementia Tindal-Carill-Worsley, with aid from the National Art-Collections Fund and government grant-in-aid administered by the Victoria and Albert Museum.

It is hard for modern Manchester people to imagine Platt Hall as a country house in the village of Rusholme, surrounded by the rural areas of Moss Side, Fallowfield and Longsight. The original design for improvements to Platt park has recently come to light. It is signed and dated by William Emes, 1768, making this his earliest dated landscape proposal. Emes (fl. 1760-85) began his career as head gardener at Kedleston, and was a close follower of 'Capability' Brown and his picturesque style. Platt Hall was originally surrounded by a boundary belt of trees (which eventually grew to support the rookery that William Royle saved from destruction in 1907). Platt Brook, now culverted, was then a wide stream, featuring prominently in the design of the southerly view. The house was enclosed from the park, and its grazing animals, by a ha-ha, or sunken fence. To the north were pleasure grounds, and to the west, where now there is a bowling green, was the kitchen garden with glass-houses. The landscaped park extended on both sides of Wilmslow Road, and covered some 300 acres.

Exterior of Platt Hall, photographed late in the 1880s.

Platt Hall interior, the drawing room, late 1880s. The fireplace by Timothy Lightoler was removed to the Worsley's town house before 1907.

Part of the park, including the ha-ha, can be seen in one or two rather naive paintings of Platt Hall, its inhabitants, and its horses. The ha-ha has now been backfilled, but its course can still be traced as an irregularity in the ground.

Perhaps one day the parkland setting of Platt Hall may be restored, like the dining room, to something of its former glory.

Thomas Worsley's Trunk

In 1954, Mrs. Clementia Tindal-Carill-Worsley (1884-1969), offered to donate a trunk of clothes worn by her great-grandfather, Thomas Carill-Worsley, to the Gallery of English Costume. Miss Anne Buck, who was then the Keeper, remembers the arrival and unpacking of the trunk as a shining moment in her career.

Thomas Worsley was born Thomas Lees in 1739, son of John Lees' first marriage. When Deborah Worsley, John Lees' second wife, succeeded her brother Peter in 1759, Thomas Worsley joined the family at Platt Hall. Immediately John Lees' plans for a new house were put in hand. John and Thomas Lees took the name Carill-Worsley, and since there were no children of the marriage, Thomas was adopted as heir to the Platt estate. He held Platt Hall for ten years, from his father's death in 1799 to his own in 1809. Thomas married Elizabeth Norman late in his life, in 1791. She survived him until 1833, having borne him five children.

Thomas Carill-Worsley thus lived for most of his life at Platt Hall; indeed as a young man in his twenties must have watched the new house being built, and even perhaps pored over the rival plans of Jupp, Carr and Lightoler. Few details of his life are known.

Like his father, he became a trustee of the non-conformist chapel at Cross Street, where the Reverend William Gaskell, husband of the novelist, became Unitarian minister in the mid 19th century. Thomas Worsley seems to have been a man of business, for a long and diligent correspondence on his lead mining holdings in Derbyshire is preserved in the Archives department of Manchester Central Reference Library. Frustratingly, no such documents are known relating to the textile interests of the Lees and Worsley families.

Thomas Worsley's trunk is large and imposing, of leather, brass-studded with arabesques and the GR royal cypher. It is lined with marbled paper, and in the lid is the maker's label: "Smith and Lucas, Coffer and Plate Case Makers to His Majesty and her Royal Highness the Princess Dowager of Wales". Inside were found seven suits and coats, mostly dating from 1760-80, and a beautiful dressing gown, or banyan, of deep green silk damask. The suits suggest that Mr. Worsley was a rather well-built man. There are also nine waistcoats, some with embroidered, and some woven patterns. Thomas Worsley's hat, made by "Jonn White Arundel Street", probably dates from the 1770's, and is of beaver covered with black silk. Boxes containing several pairs of rather plain buckles were in the trunk, together with a well-worn pair of comfortable-looking black leather shoes, marked inside "Mr. Worsley". Men seem not to be habitual hoarders of old shoes, as women are; in Platt Hall's collection of 18th century shoes, sixty pairs are women's, and just one pair belonged to a man—Mr. Worsley.

Thomas Carill Worsley's trunk
of clothes (trunk made c. 1751-75).

Perhaps the most noteworthy survival is his wig of white horsehair, complete with spare black silk wig-bags to tie up the queue of the wig.
Its pristine condition may cause second thoughts about the supposed lack of hygiene in the 18th century—unless, of course, the wig was for some reason left almost unworn.

It is unlikely that this is anything like Thomas Worsley's entire wardrobe. There are few things in the trunk of a fashion later than about 1780. Perhaps his sons or other beneficiaries were left his clothes in his will. None of his shirts, cravats, or other body linen survives. Nevertheless, the collection gives us a remarkable insight into the dress of a provincial English gentleman; usually only the elaborate court and formal dress suits, with their lavish embroidery, survive.

Mr. Thos. Worsley's green cloth suit, with gold embroidery c. 1760-80.

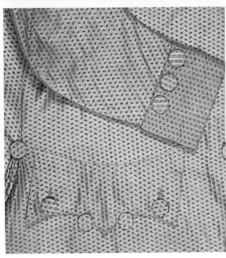

Mr. Thos. Worsley's figured silk suit c. 1760-80.

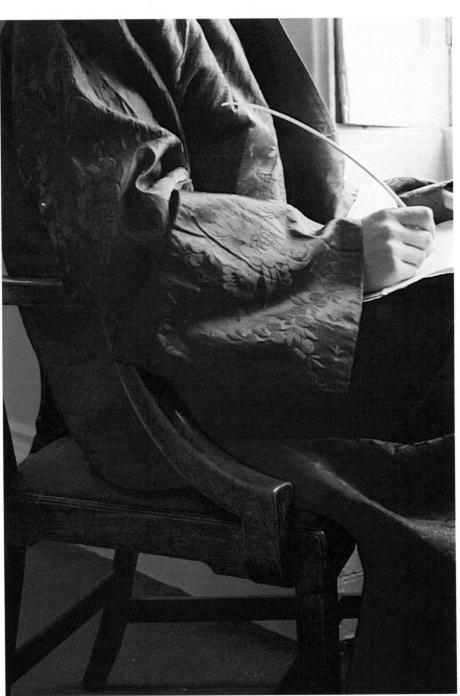

Right.
Mr. Thos. Worsley's green damask dressing gown c. 1760-80.

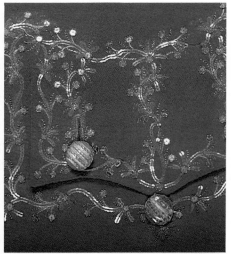

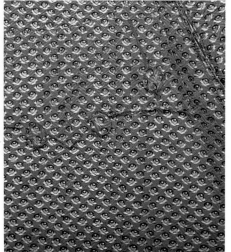

Mr. Thos. Worsley's hat, wig and wig bag c. 1770.

Mr. Thos. Worsley's purple cloth suit c. 1760-80.

Mr. Thos. Worsley's mauve figured silk suit c. 1760-90.

We can infer that the mauve cloth suit (illustrated in the chapter on the English gentleman and his tailor) was intended for daily wear, the unfashionable sleeved waistcoat being warm in cold weather.

The embroidered cloth suits would have been more formal, as would those of figured silk; while his red corded silk suit, though rich in fabric, is plainly tailored, probably for semi-formal wear. None of the suits has the elegance required for court and fashionable society formal wear, like the suits worn by Lord Stanley of Alderley, which are also featured in the chapter on tailoring.

Can we guess anything of Thomas Worsley's character from his clothes? While it is misleading to weave fantasies and legends from museum specimens, the suits suggest a gentleman in good standing. They are comfortable, their materials are of good quality, their decoration is in the mainstream of smart taste, but they are far from extravagant or ostentatiously fashionable. All is just as one would expect of a country gentleman, and looking at the propriety and soberness of his dress, one recalls the tradition of Puritanism and hard work in the Worsley family.

Hats of 1901, original drawings
by Barbara Phillipson, taken from
The Gentlewoman
May 18 1906 for *English Women's
Clothing in the Present Century*
C. W. Cunnington 1932.

The Gallery of English Costume

The Cunnington Collection.

In 1930, a middle aged doctor was passing a London antique shop, and spotted a beautiful old silk dress, which he thought might be turned into an evening cloak for his wife. He bought it very cheaply, but when they came to examine the dress at home, they could not bring themselves to cut it up until they knew at least how old it was. So they took it along to a very august museum for advice, and were told that the dress was "Victorian", perhaps dating from the 1870's. Little other information was forthcoming, and they left disappointed, under the impression that nineteenth century costume was not considered worthy of serious study.

The doctor was C. Willett Cunnington, his wife Phillis was also a physician, and though they were busy people, they accepted the challenge.
They began to buy up old fashion journals and haunted junk-shops looking for costume; they bought dresses from their patients and rummaged through charity old clothes collections. For a shilling or two they picked up dresses whose value is now measured in hundreds of pounds.

> "We were not seeking dresses that had belonged to notable persons, but those of ordinary folk, for we were concerned with mass psychology, not with the psychology of the individual".
> (*Looking Over My Shoulder* C. W. Cunnington, 1961)

Within a few years their collection was so large that they housed it in two moth and damp-proof huts, each fifty feet long, at the bottom of their garden.

Dr. Willett Cunnington built up a reputation as a lecturer and broadcaster with a flair for racy anecdote, and a gift for summing up the spirit of an age. With his wife, he embarked on a series of textbooks on costume, as well as more theoretical works on the psychology of dress.

In 1937 the monumental *English Women's Clothing in the Nineteenth Century* was published by Faber. Copiously illustrated, and spiced with numerous quotations from contemporary sources, this became a standard work. It put costume at last in its rightful place with other decorative arts, and examined fashion in its social and economic context.

The Cunningtons, with other pioneers like James Laver, made the study of dress "respectable" and helped to remove the stigma of frivolity and triviality. Nowadays no good museum would send an enquirer away with the inadequate dating "Victorian". Indeed their work has invaded almost every living room in the country—compare the dress and manners of pre-war cinema costume dramas with the meticulous research that goes into such BBC productions as *Pride and Prejudice* and *Barchester Towers*.

The Foundation of The Gallery of English Costume

At the end of *English Women's Dress in the Nineteenth Century*
Dr. Cunnington wrote:

> "Although Costume is the oldest of the Arts, and evokes a far wider
> response than any other, it is not yet considered of sufficient importance in
> this country to have a museum dedicated to its study . . . A costume
> museum, if it is to be something better than a mausoleum for old clothes,
> needs to be organised scientifically. Each specimen should be there for
> some purpose, illustrating either social or technological change . . . The
> ordinary, commonplace dress is therefore of greater scientific value than
> one which is "almost unique" or atypical."

Among the museums he had visited was Platt Hall, Manchester, then an Art
Gallery devoted to eighteenth century furniture and pictures. Here he was
impressed by "An excellent collection, admirably displayed, of some 90
dresses including types not to be seen elsewhere . . . This collection is
now rapidly increasing, and now rivals any in the country."

In 1945, the Cunningtons decided to retire from
medicine, and they offered their collection for sale. The
City of Manchester Art Galleries saw that Platt Hall,
now standing empty after the war, would make a
perfect home for it. A successful public appeal was
launched to raise the money, and the entire
Cunnington collection of about 3,500 items,
together with their magnificent library of books,
journals and photographs was purchased for Manchester.
Dr. Cunnington's cherished dream of a national museum of
costume was realised, in the city whose prosperity is founded
on the textile industry.

Miss Anne Buck OBE

Ann Buck became Platt Hall's first Keeper of Costume in 1947.
There could have been no more fortunate appointment, for her contribution to the scholarship of costume is unrivalled. Under her guidance, the collection was catalogued, stored and displayed to the highest possible standards. Dr. Cunnington's bias toward the nineteenth century, and to women's clothing, was balanced by a vigorous collecting policy, and men's and children's wear were added to the collection, together with many treasures from the seventeenth and eighteenth centuries. Miss Buck did not neglect contemporary design, and in the 1950's and early '60's the Cotton Board made several generous donations of couture dresses.

As a collection of national importance, Platt Hall has a significant role to play in research and education. Displays are lively, but informative as well, and are always grounded in thorough study of the library and collection.
A series of costume picture books is in great demand, particularly among the large numbers of schools studying costume for O- and A-level examinations. More scholarly publications have also come from Platt Hall in a steady flow. Anne Buck has numerous important publications to her credit, and her successors Christina Walkley and Vanda Foster have also produced books on costume (titles are given in our book list). There is always work in progress for publication and for exhibitions. None of this would be possible without the painstaking skills of the textile conservator, who cleans and repairs objects, not in order to make them look brand new again, but to stabilise their condition for the enjoyment and education of future generations.

Original press photograph of pink and white organdie evening dress, by Victor Stiebel at Jacqmar, for the Cotton Board, Manchester. Modelled at the Hyde Park Hotel, London 1953, and given to Platt Hall by the Cotton Board.

Platt Hall Now

Since the days of the Cunnington collection, the Gallery of English Costume has expanded rapidly. The collection now numbers some 18,000 pieces of costume, textiles and dress accessories, and the library contains about 17,500 books, journals, fashion plates, photographs, trade catalogues and documents. We try to collect clothes from all walks of life, from high fashion to working class clothing, and to look at dress in relation to social history, and to the customs and manners of the age.
There is less emphasis on the mass psychology which fascinated Dr. Cunnington, and more on the individual background of the costume. Wherever possible, notes are taken of the wearer's history, and the occasion of buying and wearing clothes.

Contemporary dress is given due recognition, and modern clothes from Mary Quant to Mothercare and Marks & Spencer, and from Zandra Rhodes and Caroline Charles to Manchester street punk are all collected. We have several Laura Ashley dresses, some worn by museum staff who give their old things to the gallery. However, we are far from complacent about our modern collection; there are several major designers whose work ought to be better represented, and the rapidly changing styles of the young are more easily captured by the video camera than collected as museum pieces. It is also important that we start to collect costume of ethnic minorities, especially since we serve an exciting cosmopolitan area of Manchester.

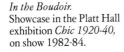

In the Boudoir.
Showcase in the Platt Hall exhibition *Chic 1920-40,* on show 1982-84.

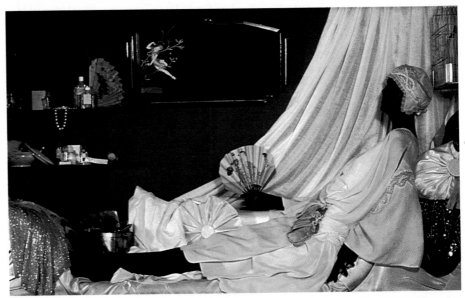

Robin Hill, 3rd year student at Manchester Polytechnic, painting a mural for the exhibition *Chic 1920-40*.

Exhibitions are changed regularly, and there is at least one major new display every year. We strive to have material from every century since 1600 on show at all times, so that schools and colleges can be fairly certain of finding material relevant to their special field of study.
The library is in constant demand by research students, though it has to be restricted to those working at degree level, and those who intend publication. T.V. and theatre designers find the library and collection a great source of information and inspiration.

Our newest venture has been our collaboration with Laura Ashley Ltd. Prints taken from the museum collection will grace the Laura Ashley shops, and in return, Mrs. Ashley has most generously undertaken the publication of this book. At the time of writing, the Gallery of English Costume, like many other local authority services, is suffering economic hardship, resulting in the curtailing of opening hours. This has particularly affected schools, and the many local visitors who regularly drop in and bring their friends. We hope that the doors of Platt Hall will soon open again all the year round. Meanwhile, Laura Ashley's enthusiastic support has ensured that the collection of English costume will reach a nationwide public.

Prints

Fast printed cottons with exotic floral designs came as a revelation to European society when they were brought back from the east by travellers. After 1600 they began to be imported to Britain on a systematic basis by the East India Company. Although the art of printing on paper was well understood, Europeans had been unable to find a way of printing on fabric so that the colours would not run. Spurred on by the clues gained from Indian prints, by the 1670s experimenters in England, Holland and France were at last able to fix their dyes by means of mordants. Cotton was most receptive to the wood-cut impressions, and with an abundant supply coming from the east, by 1700 the printed cotton trade was booming, supplying the insatiable demands of a public eager to buy the fresh and attractive new fabrics.

Block Printing from *The Useful Arts and Manufactures of Great Britain* part 1. pub. The Society for Promoting Christian Knowledge. c.1845.

Understandably, manufacturers of traditional materials began to get worried about their loss of trade, and by lobbying parliament, succeeded in getting acts passed to suppress their rivals. In 1701, the wearing of imported Indian prints was banned, and in 1721 it became illegal to wear English printed cottons. The printers were still able to export their goods, and printed linen and linen/cotton mixtures were still sold. Examples of early 18th century prints are very rare, and are usually found as linings to garments of other materials. The two opposite are the linings of stomachers, which were worn at the bodice front and show the two main dyes, which were derived from vegetable substances, madder for red, and indigo for blue. They show how simple many of the patterns were, and how different effects could be achieved. The blue floral pattern is varied by the use of a "resist"—an impervious substance which is painted on to prevent certain areas from taking up the dye.

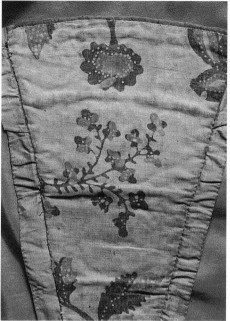

Above and left: Embroidered stomacher. Front re-used 17th century embroidery depicting the Pelican feeding her young. Back lined woodblock printed linen in indigo with resist. Early 18th century.

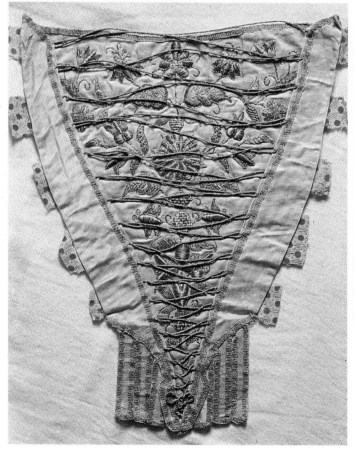

Above and left: Embroidered stomacher with crisscross gold threads and tabs for pinning to dress. Back lined loosely woven linen-cotton mix fabric woodblock printed with madder. c.1760.

1770 — 1790

Rivalry could hold back the growth of cotton printing, but not prevent it. With the inventions of the 1760s and 70s, by men such as Arkwright and Hargreaves, speeding up the processes of spinning and weaving cotton, it became cheap, and easily available. Being washable it was an ideal clothing fabric. It was clearly senseless to continue to prohibit cotton printing, and in 1774 the ban was lifted. The cotton industry was centred in Lancashire, and printers found it convenient to set up shop near the mills.

While most printing had traditionally been carried out in the London area, by the turn of the 19th century, Lancashire had taken the lead. These cottons are typical of the fabrics printed in the 1770s and 1780s, the light ground and trailing floral designs reflecting contemporary woven silks, the wobbly background dots on the monochrome print show that the medium was not completely mastered and technical difficulties remained. Occasional dots are detectable on the other prints; these were used to position the wood blocks correctly. The main pattern was printed as a dark brown outline.
A yellow from either the plant Weld, or Quercitron bark was used along with madder and indigo, broadening the palette. On these coloured prints, the blues and yellows have been "pencilled" in, that is, painted by hand.
By superimposing them, green was produced. These techniques inevitably gave a very lively effect. Prints for this period have a particular charm which was lost as the processes became more exact.

23

Woodblock printing
Left: Linen from Bed-gown c.1770
see full illustration p.51-52.
Below: Linen from Bed-gown c.1770.
Opposite page.
Left: Cotton day dress 1775-85.
The pattern is very similar to
actual woodblocks in the
Victoria and Albert Museum
said to come from a Carlisle
Print Works.
Right: Detail of fabric.

1790 — 1810

Prints from the 1790s often have a profusion of rich pattern against a very dark ground. They sometimes come as a surprise since this period is usually associated with a preference for the plain white fabrics of the "neoclassical" styles of dress. In fact, strongly contrasting colours were often used for accessories such as bags, shawls and hats. In the printed cottons of the time, the same colours are seen, particularly rich reds and ochres which became popular following the discovery of Pompeian wall paintings. The fabric below comes from a dress that was obviously a favourite. It was originally made in the style of the 1790s, then the waist was raised to follow the current fashions of the next decade. Its darkness would not have been out of place; some fabrics were still being produced with this type of colour combination, although in more stylised, regimented patterns. The dress opposite dates from about 1805. More characteristic of the years 1800-1810 was the so-called "Drab-style" in which paler browns, olives and yellows predominated. It is seen here in an abstract tree design printed on a beautifully draping soft cotton twill, of about 1805-7.

Woodblock printing 1790-1810
Opposite page: Darkground
print from stout cotton dress
originally made in the 1790s but
altered 1800-1810.
Left: Soft cotton twill dress
printed in "drab style" colours
1805-7.
Below: Dark ground print stout
cotton dress c.1806.

Roller Printing

High quality printing by means of engraved copper plates had been carried out since the mid 18th century. In an attempt to reproduce the sharp clear lines of the copper plate by a cheaper method, in 1783, Thomas Bell took out a patent for a way of printing from engraved metal rollers.

From the 1790s onwards, roller printing was used by Lancashire mills to produce dress fabrics. It was confined to cheap prints in small monochrome patterns, often with an emphasis on a stripe. The dress opposite, dating from about 1815 was roller printed. The tiny dotted pattern, known as a "machine ground" could only be made by metal rollers. At about this time, roller printing expanded and larger patterns began to be designed. Eventually, roller printing almost entirely surplanted the old wood blocks.

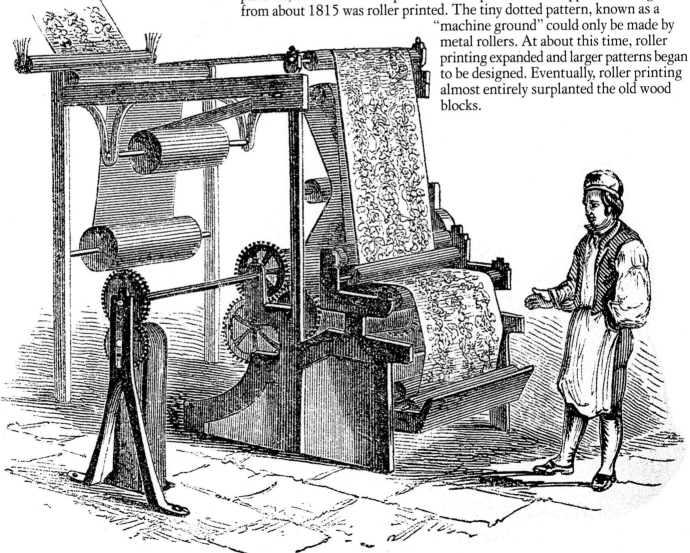

Cylinder printing. *The Useful Arts and Manufactures of Great Britain* Part 1.
The Society for promoting Christian Knowledge c.1845.

Fine cotton dress with roller printed design 1810-15. Said to have been worn by one of the Clarke family, farmers of Irlam, Cheshire.

Cylinder or Roller Printing

As many as eight colours may be applied at the same time, by having as many engraved rollers, each with its accompanying colour-trough, etc., revolving against the iron drum. The greatest nicety of arrangement is required to bring all these rollers to print the cloth at the precise spots required, but when once properly adjusted, each may be made to deposit its colour on the calico with certainty and regularity. When the calico is printed, it is dried by being drawn through a long gallery or passage, which is commonly heated by the flue of a furnace which extends the whole length of the floor of the gallery.

The upper surface of the gallery is covered with rough cast-iron plates, which become quickly heated, and present a good radiating surface. A piece of calico, of twenty-eight yards, is usually drawn through the gallery in about two minutes. The length of the printing roller may vary, according to the breadth of the calico to be printed, from thirty to forty inches; its diameter may be from four to six inches, or even a foot. Each roller is bored, and accurately turned, from a solid piece of metal.

The Useful Arts and Manufactures of Great Britain Part 1. The manufacture of Woven Goods. Part III—Calico Printing. p.13/14

1820—1830

The development of more elaborate roller prints is evident in cotton dresses from the 1820s with bold patterns, which are still, however, often based on stripes. The red and blue dress is particularly interesting because the stripes are printed on the cross grain of the fabric. New bright, clear colours were beginning to be available such as chrome yellow, prussian blue and a solid green. "Turkey Red" grounds were particularly popular, especially combined with yellow patterns. This example is in excellent condition; usually the colour combination fades with age. Called Turkey Red because the method was derived from practices in the near East, the clear colour was created from madder by a process which involved soaking the cloth in oil and soda.
The paler stripes are produced by discharging, removing the colour after dyeing.
Another good example dating from the late 1830s, is shown on the next pages alongside a dress with a chrome yellow ground from the 1820s. Yellow is often found in a faded condition, since the dye is unstable.

Dress printed on fine cotton 1823-5.

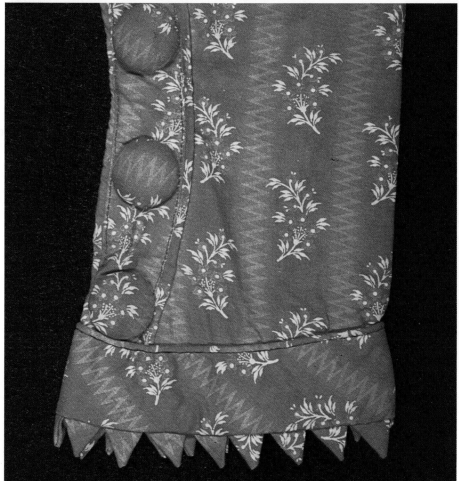

Cotton dress printed in Turkey Red
with a zigzag stripe in the lighter
shade and a discharge printed
yellow sprig c.1825.
Said to have been worn by Mrs. Taylor
of Newcroft, Urmston, Lancs.

Printed cotton dress 1822-4.

Page from a cotton printer's pattern book from a print works at Rossendale near Manchester dating from the 1820s. This is one of a number of such books from the firm in the Platt Hall collection. Some show the firm's own designs while others are collections of rivals' designs, many of which are French.

Above: Figure left: Cotton dress in Turkey red, printed with yellow and black feathers. c.1837-40. Figure right: Fine striped muslin dress in yellow printed with brown sprigs on resist white ground 1825-30. Worn by Agnes Ewart.

White cotton dress printed with delicate floral trails. c.1826-8.

1830 — 1840

By 1830, delicate floral prints and light grounds predominated once again. Patterns based on stripes continued to flourish, and an added dimension was often given to the pattern by a stripe being woven into the fine cotton ground. Many prints were inspired by the angular floral patterns on woven shawls imported from the east, or made in Paisley. One of the dresses at Platt Hall incorporates another exotic motif in its purple and yellow design, Egyptian hieroglyphics. We were very fortunate to come across by chance a fashion plate featuring a similar material. Unusual flowers, grasses and ferns were tremendously popular, as were sinuous coral designs. The elegant grass pattern shown opposite features the new solid green. The anemone pattern in green and red is printed on a cream challis, a mixture of silk and wool much favoured at the time. With printing now a more exact process and the colours easier to create, designers no longer used dark outlines, and were able to adopt a more fluid, painterly approach.

Dress in fine striped muslin printed with exotic patterns including Egyptian Hieroglyphs c.1837. Fabric similar to that in fashion plate for *La Belle Assemblée* June 1829.

Top: Cream challis dress printed with red anemones. Going-away dress of Miss F. S. Shuffrey 1837.
Centre: Left figure: Striped muslin dress printed in shawl-type patterns 1837-39. Right figure: striped muslin dress printed with grasses 1837-9.
Below: Green and white striped printed muslin dress 1833-5

1840—1850

Floral and shawl pattern prints on light grounds continued through the 1840s, but there was a tendency for the designs to become smaller and less imposing. The Victorian era of mass production was well under way and mill-owners, to satisfy the huge demand from new markets for a constant supply of novelties, turned out many variations of tried and trusted themes. The floral pattern below is very simply drawn, with the ever popular coral pattern and machine ground included.

As a striking alternative to such delicate prettiness, many of the heavier cottons were printed with bold, jazzy patterns which demonstrate some interesting uses of shading by discharge and resist processes. In the dress opposite, made in the 1850s from a printed wool of the late 1840s, the effect of the lace pattern superimposed on checks over a shaded brown and purple ground seems to deny the surface of the fabric.

Right: Striped muslin dress printed with floral and coral stripes with machine ground 1845-50.

Striped muslin dress printed with small flowers c.1840.

Top left: Stout cotton dress printed with pink and red floral striped pattern c.1845.

Top right: Stout cotton dress printed with red and brown striped pattern c.1845.

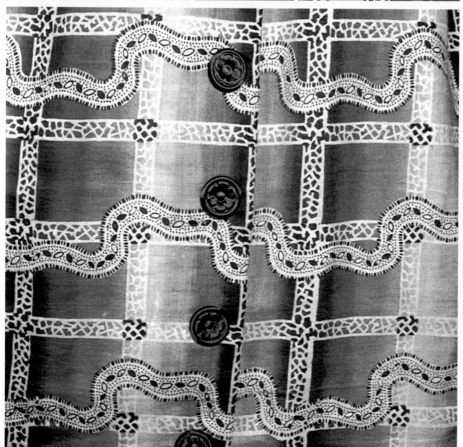

Left: Cream wool dress printed in green brown and purple lace and check pattern. Fabric 1847-50. Dress 1850-55. The shaded grounds of these fabrics are created by a resist process.

1850 — 1860

In general the 1850s was not a decade characterised by a love of bold dress fabrics. Perhaps because dresses themselves were becoming much wider, supported by the crinoline and extensively flounced, pattern was to some extent subservient to texture. Layers of fine gauzy muslin were worn to great effect, and these were enhanced by all over surface patterns in pastel pinks or mauves, printed in monochrome over a woven check.

Very often muslins were printed *à disposition*, with a specially designed border print intended for skirt flounces, and a narrower complementary border to decorate the bodice. These came in innumerable designs, but most popular were Paisley type patterns derived from Indian shawls. Copying other textiles had always been a useful source of new ideas for cotton printers. The dress above incorporates large Paisley pine cones alternated with full blown roses above a tartan border. The body of the fabric is decorated with rosebuds. The pink fabric below is printed to look like gingham, with a border print resembling a woven silk ribbon. On this, naturalistically depicted roses are shown as if they were "clouded", that is, printed only on the warp thread, to give a blurred effect.

Such eclecticism and naturalistic treatment of motifs have often been cited as evidence of a decline in standards at this time. In consequence, textile historians have frequently ignored or dismissed printed cottons of the mid-Victorian period. The difference between designs from the late 18th century and those of the 1850s should not be seen as a decline from an absolute standard so much as a change to a completely different approach. By the mid-century, the scale of textile production had increased immeasurably. Instead of manufacturing goods for a small, relatively prosperous section of society, the new customer was poorer, and demanded pretty fabrics which were as cheap as possible. Certainly the dresses produced in the 1850s are very attractive indeed. Manufacturers at this time did care about the appearance of their products, but not just those destined for rich people. This is shown in *The Journal of Designs and Manufactures,* a fascinating publication which ran from 1849-1851. Alongside descriptions of the sort of candelabra and vases which were to grace the halls of the great Exhibition of 1851, could be found actual examples of fabrics. Some were elaborate, but many more were humble prints. In November 1849, a piece of purple printed calico by Thomas Hoyle and Sons of Manchester was included. Hoyle's prints were very well known as serviceable fabrics. Mrs. Gaskell's *Mary Barton,* a poor Manchester dressmaker of the 1840s, was described as wearing one.

The Journal of Design wrote:
> "This graceful design, with its tiny red dots, is a slight departure from the ordinary style of the Mayfield Works. We are apt to associate the Hoyle purple with the humbler class of weaves, but the present pattern is such a successful union of quiet grace and liveliness, that it might, we think, be worn by all or any who are not too grand to use a calico print. A ribbon of bright light blue, amber, or cherry colour, at the wearer's neck, would be a harmonious combination."
> (p.108 *Journal of Design.* No. 9. November 1849)

Check muslin dress with border
print in purple c.1855.

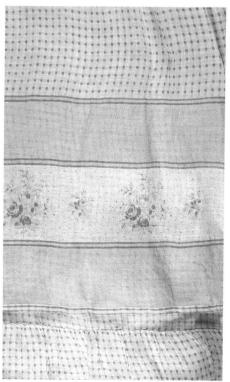

Muslin dress with check print
and border pattern in pink c.1855.

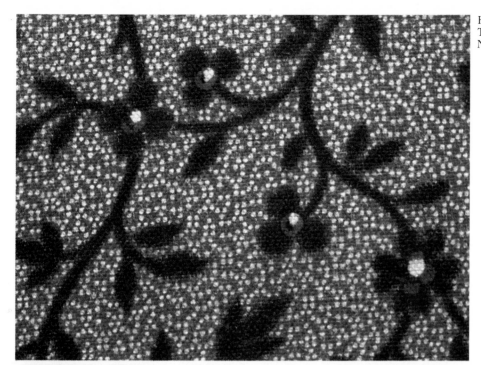

Hoyles printed calico from
The *Journal of Design* No. 9
November 1849.

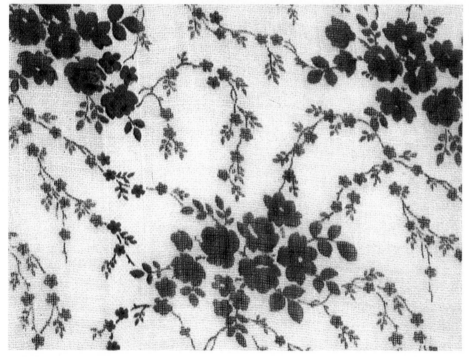

Check weave muslin
dress printed with brown floral
pattern c.1857.

Opposite page:
Hand-coloured fashion plate
from *The World of Fashion*
September 1852 showing a
printed dress on the left.

Home for the easter holidays in 1856, a student called William Perkin was carrying out some experiments and produced a vivid purple dye, a derivative of coal-tar, which he christened Mauveine. The discovery made his fortune, and wrought a revolution in the textile world. The rich deep colour produced by this first synthetic dye was an immediate success. Other brilliant coal-tar dyes quickly followed, such as magenta, and bright blue. These revived the taste for bright colours. Silk took the dyes especially well, and many surviving dresses from the 1860s are wonderfully vibrant. Perhaps because of this new interest in colour, and perhaps as a reaction to the delicate little patterns of the previous decade, printed cottons of the 1860s once more have splendidly bold designs, executed with great inventiveness.

Top: Very fine check woven
muslin with pink stripes and
resist printed rose pattern 1860-3.
Middle left: Cotton printed with
mauve floral pattern 1865-70
worn by a Manchester woman.
Middle right: Stout cotton printed
with geometric border print in
dark red 1860-65.

Far left: Morning gown in white
cotton with printed green stripe
c.1865 worn by a Mrs. Weetman,
who was born in 1844.
Left: Details from above gown
and dress shown on p83. c.1865.

Provincial Women in the Eighteenth Century

Fashionable Society

Ladies in the Dress of 1784 from *The Ladies' Own Memorandum Book*
"*1783, November 20* At Chases (Norwich) for 2 Ladies Pocket Books pd. 0.2.0.
1783, November 21 Gave Nancy one of the Ladies Pocket Books for 1784. Gave her also a pretty pocket Leather Inkhorn"
(Parson Woodforde's Diary, recording gifts to his niece).

In Platt Hall library is a manuscript in marbled paper covers: "An Inventory of Part of the Household Furniture, Wardrobe of Apparell, Laces, Diamonds, China and Table Linen, late the property of Mrs. Mary Gilpin, deceas'd. Taken and appraised the 4th Day of August 1785."

The list runs to some 340 items or sets of items, to a total of £220 worth of clothing and £320.2.0 in jewellery, buckles, smelling bottles, toothpick cases and the like. It begins:

"A Laylock sattin gown unmade
a pair of stays
a new pr. of do.
a Waiscoat
Ten Leno Aprons
ten handkerchiefs
a box with Artificial flowers
Ten fine Ostrich feathers
Thirty-five pair of Colour'd and black Lady's embroidered Shoes . . ."

The inventory includes nearly fifty dresses:
". . . a rich Stone colour Tabby gown trimmed with Ermine
a rich pink Sattin Pettycoat
a neat green ground flowerd Lutestring gown and Coat trimmed
a very rich and elegant white Sattin Gown and Coat full trimmed with rich silk fringe
a yellow and purple striped Sattin gown and coat
a striped Lutestring gown and Coat trimmed
a very rich and beautiful Laylock Sattin gown and Coat
a very neat chintz Pattern and Striped fine Callico Poloneze gown and Coat trimmed . . ."

A "gown and coat" at this period meant a robe worn open over a petticoat, the usual style for most of the eighteenth century. A "poleneze" or polonaise gown was worn with the skirts puffed up over a petticoat, and was very fashionable from about 1770-85.

Mary Gilpin's inventory was signed by Hassell Hutchins and Richard Sadleir of King Street, Covent Garden, and apparently represents the accumulated wardrobe of a wealthy lady in fashionable London society. Her lace alone would have been worth a considerable sum. Yet even if we assume that Mary Gilpin was rich, the size of her wardrobe at her death causes some surprise. We have probably been told that in the eighteenth century people rarely changed their clothes, even that they were "sewn into them".

We can all remember schoolbooks illustrated with caricatures of exaggerated and unhygienic fashions like hooped petticoats and high powdered coiffures. But despite the excesses of fops and fine ladies, clothes were taken very seriously; they represented a considerable financial investment, and were expected to wear well and retain their quality.

Nowadays the labour involved in making a tailored suit or a couture dress is probably more expensive than the materials used. In the eighteenth century the reverse was true, the fabric was the greater part of the price of a dress. Attitudes to clothing were therefore quite different, there was no "throwaway" mentality. That is why the making of inventories was so important; the wardrobes of the dead had a high financial value.
Mrs. Gilpin's clothes would have had a ready market second-hand, or would, more likely, have been divided in her will. Numerous wills survive giving, in meticulous detail, bequests of clothing to relations, friends, servants and poor dependants. Each beneficiary's share would be carefully chosen to fit her social status as well as the degree of affection in which she was held.

"... a striped Lutestring gown ..."

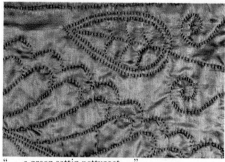

"... a green sattin pettycoat ..."

"... a rich brocaded flower'd Gown ..."

Fashionable society in *The Gardens of Carleton-House with Neapolitan Ballad Singers* Design'd 18th May 1784 from a drawing by H. W. Bunbury (1750-1811).

Robe of brown watered and damasked silk, worn with a quilted petticoat of ivory satin, and a muslin handkerchief. A typical informal gown from 1750-60.

Platt Hall has about 85 eighteenth century dresses, most dating from 1760 onwards. If you open a wardrobe and contemplate the rows of robes, the most striking thing is the beauty and quality of the materials. Silks have a rich lustre and a crispness that still drapes elegantly after two centuries. Even the printed linens and cottons of the commoner sorts of clothing have more body than many modern fabrics, and they are often richly coloured and patterned.

A high proportion of these dresses have been altered during the wearer's lifetime, and several more have been cut up in later years for fancy dress and theatrical costume. Such remodelling was a comparatively easy matter, as robes are shapes by pleating and draping, with the minimum of complicated cutting. Pleats could be unpicked and rearranged, and trimmings changed, without great damage to the fabric. Dresses of this period are stitched with large running stitches, in contrast to the delicate needlework on shirts and undergarments which were not habitually altered, and were expected to last a long time.

Mrs. Mary Gilpin's "laylock sattin gown unmade" would consist of lengths of lilac silk, carefully unpicked and smoothed, the trimmings removed and folded, and laid by in her clothes chest awaiting refashioning. Many of her fifty dresses would be outmoded and ready for similar treatment.

There are contemporary accounts of the alteration of dresses:

1790

"DECEM. 11, SATURDAY . . . Gave Nancy this morning a green silk damask Gown, that was formerly my poor Aunt Parrs . . .

DECEM. 25 SATURDAY and Christmas Day . . . Nancy having herself new made the late green Silk Gown I gave her wore it this Day for the 1st time" (The Rev. James Woodforde *The Diary of a Country Parson).*

Nancy was Parson Woodforde's niece. Aunt Parr died in 1771, so the green damask was at least nineteen years old.

In the next pages we show a small selection of women's clothes, all of which have at least a fragmentary historical background, so that we can draw some conclusions about the social background and way of life of the wearer.

Back view of an informal gown, in yellow silk, showing marks and joins where the dress has been altered 1770-80.

Yellow Brocade Dress

Detail of yellow brocade wedding dress, showing trimming on stomacher.

Said to be the wedding dress of Bertha Marjor who married Thomas Flemming in 1774.

This dress is an open robe, worn with a matching petticoat and stomacher. The stomacher fills in the opening at the bodice front and is pinned into place over the heavily boned stays. Such a dress is commonly called a sack-back robe, for the fullness of the back is held in two double box pleats which sweep in an unbroken line to the ground.

The fabric is a yellow/ivory shot silk, woven with ivory stripes and small brocaded flowers in pink, blue and green. Trimmings of pleated silk on the robe and petticoat are padded with cotton waste, and edged with matching braid. A small side hoop (pocket hoop) would support the skirts.

Wedding clothes of the eighteenth century were not always white. Though silver and white were thought seemly, and were a popular combination, white weddings were not yet an established tradition. There are four other known eighteenth century wedding dresses at Platt Hall; two are blue and white, and two are pink.

Dress for the first appearance at church on the Sunday after the wedding was as important as the wedding clothes themselves. The ceremony itself might be a quiet affair, but for the "appearance" a crowd of well-wishers and sightseers would gather. Formal visits to neighbours and friends would be made in the weeks after a marriage, and the wedding clothes would be used for best wear.

Platt Hall's earliest wedding dress, dated 1743, is said to have been worn at the York Assemblies afterwards.

Similar dresses are said to have used twenty to twenty-two yards of silk, usually about twenty inches wide. Flowered silks had a wide price range; perhaps this one cost eleven or thirteen shillings, but we cannot be sure.

LADIES DRESS FOR APRIL

FULL DRESS . . . Sacks, slight strip'd and flower'd figur'd silks, or pale colours trimmed with gauze and flowers—
—Trimmings large puffs- Down the sides of the sack one flounce all round. Sattin slippers, embroidered, with gold diamond roses, or small buckles- heels diminished in height . . . Ruffles not so deep, very shallow before and tied up with ribbons."

The Lady's Magazine April 1774.

Mrs. Flemming's yellow brocade
wedding dress 1774.

Ladies in the dress of 1774, and head-dresses for 1774,
from *The Ladies' Own Memorandum Book*.

Marriage Arrangements

*. . . New cloaths are as necessary to a bride as
the wedding ring, and if dress is ever in any
estimation at all, it certainly is on the
wedding day. . .*
*It was disputed whether (Priscilla) should
dress in a sack or a nightgown, in a Polonese
or a Brunswic. . .*
*the polonese was preferred with this proviso-
that Priscilla should make her appearance in
full dress—and visit in a negligee, and
receive her morning visits in a nightgown.*

(from the serial "A Sentimental Journey—by
a Lady" in *The Lady's Magazine*,
June 1776 p285).

Two Open Robes

Pink Silk Open Robe c.1770-80

This dress was worn by a member of the Clarke family, farmers from Irlam, Cheshire, and is said to have been a wedding dress.

It has matching pinked sleeve ruffles, and plain round cuffs, and there are narrow pleated trimmings at the neck. The fronts of the bodice meet edge to edge, so that no stomacher is needed, the dress is simply pinned together. No matching petticoat has survived; it is more than likely that there never was one, a contrasting petticoat of quilted silk being worn instead.

This style of dress, with its back pleats stitched down, was called a "nightgown". Such dresses were used for good informal wear by gentlewomen, for receiving visitors at home, and domestic portraits of Englishwomen often show women in silk dresses with quilted petticoats and white aprons presiding at tea.

Someone lower in the social scale, a farmer's wife like Mrs. Clarke, for example, would regard this as a best dress. If this was indeed a wedding dress it would have been seen at church and on special occasions afterwards.

We have photographed the dress with a neck handkerchief of green silk, embroidered with coloured silks. Such a handkerchief might have been embroidered at home. Accessories of this sort were often given as presents, and would have been prized by their owners. The muslin apron, embroidered with drawn threadwork, also belonged to the Clarke family, and was "worn for church".

Imagine Mrs. Clarke, newly married, in a country church, in her fine pink dress, with snowy white apron, cap and handkerchief. Perhaps she wears a round straw hat, and has a cardinal cloak against the weather.

Such light, lustrous silks were called "lutestrings" or "lustrings". A nightgown might take between seven and nine yards at perhaps 5/6 a yard.

Printed Linen Open Robe c.1770-80

The fabric is a crisp white linen block printed with lilac stripes, and small sprigs of red berries and green leaves. The red and green colours are "pencilled", that is to say they are painted in by hand, using a fine brush.

This dress also belonged to the Clarkes of Irlam, and is in "nightgown" form identical to the pink silk wedding dress. It was almost certainly worn by the same woman, since it is of similar size and sewn in the same manner. The wearer must have had very neat taste in dress, and it is possible that she

Mrs. Clarke's pink silk gown c.1770-80.

had this dress made at the same time as her wedding dress, to suit her new way of life.

If the pink silk was for "best" or smart informal wear, this dress would have been used for morning dress, for light housework and needlework, as the linen was a good washable fabric. Sir Peter Teazle, in *The School for Scandal* (1777), reminds his wife that before he married her, and elevated her to London society, she was ". . . the daughter of a plain country squire. Recollect, Lady Teazle, when I first saw you sitting at your tambour, in a pretty figured linen gown with a bunch of keys at your side."

Detail of pink gown and embroidered green silk handkerchief.

Detail of linen gown and muslin handkerchief, embroidered with drawn threadwork.

Detail of Mrs. Clarke's white muslin apron "worn for church".

A New Pattern for an Apron or Handkerchief, from the *Lady's Magazine* 1785.

Mrs. Clarke's printed linen gown c.1770-80.

Such dresses were often passed down to maidservants for best wear, and were a common sight at country churches:

1784

"OCTOBER 12 . . . Married my old Maid Eliz. Claxton to Charles Cary . . . She was dressed in a Linnen Gown that my Niece gave her some time back." (The Rev. James Woodforde *The Diary of a Country Parson*).

The dress is photographed with a handkerchief of muslin with drawn thread embroidery. This "Dresden work" is much stronger than lace, and was used for garments in daily use. Lace and muslin were also passed on to servants, and "suits" of Dresden work (caps, aprons, handkerchiefs, sleeve ruffles) were often mentioned in wills.

Printed linens might cost 3/- to 3/6 a yard, and seven or eight yards would be needed for a gown.

Printed Linen Bed-gown

c.1760-70

The bed-gown is a simple garment, with kimono-like sleeves, and is generously gored to wrap round the hips.

Printed linen and woven checked lining material.

A three-quarter length wrapping gown with wide gores at the hips. It comes from the Aldersey family of the hamlet of Aldersey in Cheshire, where they are said to have lived as country squires at Aldersey Hall (now demolished) since the 13th century.

The fabric is a white linen, block printed in indigo blue with a design of trailing flowers and dots, probably produced by the sophisticated "China blue" dyeing technique. It is lined with two patterns of woven linen check.

This particular gown shows little sign of wear. Perhaps it belonged to the servant of a well-to-do family who might have worn it for the rougher work of a country household; or perhaps it was worn, as its name suggests, as a kind of dressing jacket.

However, the bed-gown was primarily a countrywoman's garment, a loose wrapping jacket worn over a petticoat of wool, linen or linsey-woolsey. It had no fastenings, being secured about the waist by the apron strings. A handkerchief was usually worn at the neck, perhaps of gay Manchester cotton, and the apron might be pinned up for carrying things. This style of dress is to be seen in many paintings of kitchen and dairy maids, and field labourers; the most famous is Stubbs' *The Haymakers* at the Tate Gallery.

Mill-workers in Lancashire wore cotton bed-gowns and might have had the price of a bed-gown deducted from their wages. Samuel Bamford (1788-1872) recalled his mother's ordinary dress in his Lancashire childhood:

> "Her dark hair was combed over a roll before and behind and confined by a mob cap as white as bleached linen could be made, her neck covered with a handkerchief, over which she wore a bed-gown; and a clean checked apron with black hose and shoes completed her attire."

while his Methodist aunt:

> "... took snuff, wore a mob-cap, a bed-gown, a stiff pair of stays which stood out at the bosom, a warm woollen petticoat, white knitted hose, and shoes with patten clogs to keep her feet warm."

By the 1790's the fashion for stiff-boned stays had died out in city society, and high waisted dresses were the new look. But the eighteenth century country dress lingered on in secluded rural areas. When Lady Llanover saw the bed-gown in remote parts of Wales, she concluded that this must be a local tradition, and in the Welsh cultural renaissance of the 1830's and 40's the notion of a Welsh national costume was born.

Wensley Dale Knitters, from
The Costume of Yorkshire,
George Walker 1814.

Printed linen bed-gown
c.1760-70.

WENSLEY DALE KNITTERS

*Simplicity and industry characterize
the manners and occupations of the
various humble inhabitants of
Wensley Dale. Their wants, it is true,
are few; but to supply these, almost
constant labour is required. In any
business where the assistance of the
hands is not necessary, they
universally resort to knitting.
Young and old, male and female,
are all adepts in this art.
Shepherds attending their flocks, men
driving cattle, women going to
market, are all thus industriously and
doubly employed. A woman of the
name of Slinger, who lived in
Cotterdale, was accustomed regularly
to walk to the market at Hawes, a
distance of three miles, with the
weekly knitting of herself and family
packed in a bag upon her head,
knitting all the way. She continued
her knitting while she staid at Hawes,
purchasing the little necessaries for
her family, with the addition of
worsted for the work of the ensuing
week; all of which she placed upon
her head, returning occupied with her
needles as before. She was so
expeditious and expert, that the
produce of the day's labour was
generally a complete pair of men's
stockings.*

The Costume of Yorkshire George
Walker (1814)

Countrywoman's scarlet woollen cloak, possibly a wedding cloak, from Mobberley, Cheshire, c.1800.

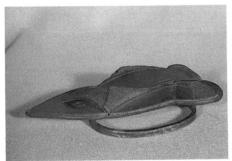

A patten, or wooden overshoe mounted on an iron ring. These were worn by countrywomen on miry roads, and for wet indoor work like washing.
In Bath, a rainy city, even fashionable women wore pattens.

Doll, dressed as a countrywoman knitting, c.1840. Note her bed-gown and petticoat. She may represent a Yorkshire daleswoman, or perhaps a fisherwoman knitting a guernsey.

53

Scarlet Cloak

c. 1800

Family tradition states that this cloak, from Mobberley in Cheshire, is a wedding garment. It is of scarlet woollen cloth, milled to make it more weatherproof, and the hood and collar are lined with two shades of red silk, the collar lining being quilted. The hood is under the collar so that it cannot be worn up without drawing the warm collar snugly round the face.

Hooded cloaks (riding hoods) were the usual wear outdoors for all women; only riding dress had tailored coats. Scarlet cloth became so popular for rural wear that this is one of the few English garments that can be called traditional. The rich red must have flattered country complexions and brightened up dark days, as Samuel Bamford noticed:

> "An ample crimson or scarlet cloak of finest wool, double milled, and of an intense dye that threw a glimmer wherever it moved, was put on, the hood being thrown over the head, cap handkerchief and all and drawn closely and comfortably round the face or left open as the wearer chose."

Many foreign travellers noticed the charm and picturesque appearance of the red cloak, and the cleanliness of countrywomen's linen.

The silk lining of the cloak suggests that it is of specially good quality, bearing out the story that it was a bride's cloak. It would be typical Sunday best for an English village woman from the mid-eighteenth to the early nineteenth century. After that date, the younger element were more likely to wear mantles, pelisses and shawls, and the scarlet cloak became an old woman's garment by the 1830's. It was adopted as a quaint survival into the costume of various charitable foundations, such as the Trinity Hospital, Castle Rising, Norfolk.

Very few scarlet cloaks survive today. Though they were common, they were so useful that they were probably worn and passed on until they were not worth keeping. However, they survive in miniature as part of the traditional dress of pedlar dolls, a popular plaything in the first half of the nineteenth century.

The scarlet cloak was also worn by country gentry. In the recently published sketchbook of Diana Sperling, a young lady of Dynes Hall in Essex, we see Diana and her sisters wearing scarlet cloaks for donkey riding, gardening, and walking to dinner with the neighbours.

A shop at Norwich, in 1785, had scarlet "cardinals" in stock, costing 10s, 12s or 15s for women, and 5s for girls.

Sarah Thrifty, licensed hawker, a pedlar doll in bed-gown and red cloak. c.1820.

LIST OF ARTICLES
sold by
SARAH THRIFTY
LICENSED HAWKER

needles cotton tape
bobbin pins sewing silk
thread worsted berlin wool
buttons stay laces purses
bracelets babies' socks stockings
garters pockets nightcap
hoods lace kettle holders
ribbon pincushions d'oyleys
knives and forks combs
perfumery stationery &c &c &c

The English Gentleman and his Tailor

While the French court sought to maintain standards established in the reign of Louis XIV, the nobility being encouraged to live among and form part of the splendours of Versailles, the English system of parliamentary democracy allowed the English nobility and gentry to lead independent lives on their own country estates. They farmed the land, went hunting and shooting, and travelled for pleasure as much to the local market towns as to the metropolis. The wealth of many families was as often increased by revenue from the new coalmines or textile mills being built on their land, as by advantageous marriages.

The outdoor life led by such men called not for the glittering luxury of silk and lace, but for stout clothing made from England's excellent wool by the expert English tailors. While the old standards were retained for occasions such as appearances at court, comfortable frock-coats were increasingly preferred to stiff, formal suits. At first the frock-coat had been a casual garment worn for sport, but by the 1770s a smart version was being used for everyday wear. The plates opposite show such a frock-coat, worn by Thomas Carill Worsley, who lived at Platt Hall.

Such coats conveyed an image of elegant simplicity especially when worn with stout buckskin breeches, top boots, a beaver hat, masses of fine linen, and an unpowdered loose hairstyle. It was a casually graceful "look" which accorded well with the now widely held view that the well-bred gentleman should exhibit restraint and good taste. This type of dress was particularly admired by the French aristocracy, to whom it made a refreshing change from their traditional formality. Moreover, in the years leading up to the French revolution, it came to be seen as a symbol of English democracy, and the wearing of it as a statement of political opposition to the Ancient Régime. By the turn of the century, English dressing was high fashion in Paris, and, through Paris, as the centre of the fashionable world, it was rapidly taken up by gentlemen throughout Europe. So well did it accord with the spirit of the age, that once adopted, this restrained style set a pattern for male dress which remained for the next two hundred years.

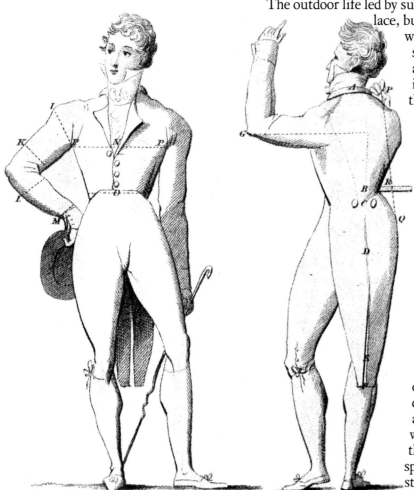

From Hearn's *Rudiments of Cutting Coats etc.* 1819 Plate 1: On Measuring.

Lilac cloth suit with velvet collar, silver covered
bone buttons and silver braid 1760-70.
Belonged to Thomas Carill Worsley 1739-1809
who lived at Platt Hall 1759-1809.

Title page from Hearn's *Rudiments of Cutting
Coats etc.* Printed and sold by the author 1819.

HEARN's
Rudiments
OF
CUTTING COATS, &c.
OF ALL SIZES,
TO FIT THE HUMAN FORM,
BY
ANATOMICAL PROPORTIONS,
IN CONJUNCTION WITH
Geometrical Principles.

PART THE FIRST.

THIRD EDITION.
WITH ADDITIONS, AND MANY VALUABLE IMPROVEMENTS.

London:
PRINTED FOR AND SOLD BY THE AUTHOR,
No. 13, *Crown Court, Little Russell Street, Covent Garden;*
SOLD ALSO, BY HIS APPOINTMENT, BY
Mr. DENHAM, 6, Great Windmill Street, Haymarket; W. TURNBULL,
Glasgow; PETER HILL and Co. Edinburgh; HODGES and M'ARTHUR,
21, College Green, Dublin; W. RUSH, Ipswich; J. CARUAC, 53, Black-
man Street, Southwark; PRESTON and WEST, Nottingham; SHERWOOD,
NEELY and Co. Paternoster-row, and J DAVIS, Stationer, 102, Minories.
Price Three Shillings, stitched.

1819.

One man who above all others was responsible for the transformation of this country style into the respectable dress of the male establishment was George Brummell (1778-1840). Of comparatively humble origins, he rose to mingle with the greatest in society, through his belief that gentlemanly behaviour could make any man the fit companion of a prince, regardless of background. Brummell's ideal was particularly expressed through his appearance, which gave the effect of exquisite simplicity, belying the hard work needed for its creation. He demanded perfection in every aspect of his attire, from his lustrous boots to his pristine white linen, its crispness enhanced by the judicious application of starch. He would spend hours achieving the deceptively simple knot of his cravat. A visitor who saw his valet carrying an armful of linen through the hall, upon enquiry was told that "Those, Sir, are our failures."

Most important of all, Brummell relied upon the high quality fabric and smooth, glovelike fit of his outergarments to complete the effect.

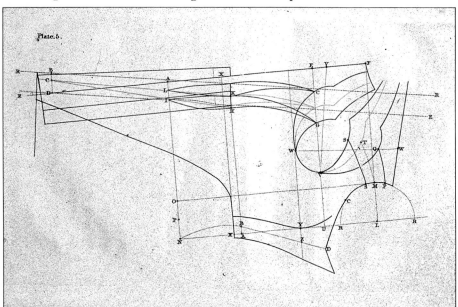

Plates on cutting from Hearn's *Rudiments of Cutting Coats etc.* Printed and sold by the author 1819.

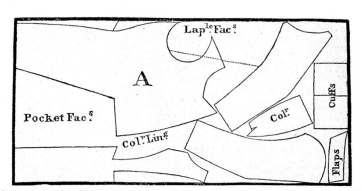

A It will be found in large size coats for very short men, there will not be sufficient width to get the cuffs out as marked; in that case take one of the cuffs out where the flaps are marked, and take the flaps off the bottom of pocket facings; and when the width of the cloth will not admit of the collar lining to be taken out as marked, it must come out at the top of inside sleeve. You may, in some cases, find your lappel facings will answer best taken out where the cuffs and collar is marked; when such is the case, take one of the cuffs out of the sie piece, and the other above it, as in plate D, and placing the top of the inside sleeve as near to the cuff as possible, and you will find the collar will come out with the lappel facings. In some sizes your pocket facings will allow you to take the collar off at the bottom.

To this end, he patronized three different tailors, for his coat, waistcoat and breeches respectively. The capacity of woollen cloth to be stretched and moulded to the figure was a major reason why it became such a popular fabric for men's dress. Since English tailors had been making woollen country clothes throughout the 18th century, it was small wonder that, when wool began to be generally fashionable, it was to English tailors that gentlemen flocked from all over Europe, to gain the benefit of their traditional expertise.

The increased use of tailored woollen garments led to rapid developments in tailoring skills. Not content with their old "rule of thumb" methods of cutting and fitting, tailors began to study anatomy and geometry, in order to discover a really scientific system which would enable them to calculate a perfect fit no matter how peculiar the customer's shape. In the early years of the century, London tailors raced to publish their own particular cutting system, each one claiming to be better than the last. One such work is in the Platt Hall collection, the 1819 edition of Hearn's *Rudiments of Cutting Coats etc. of all*

Retracting tape measure hand painted in nails and inches on glazed linen tape in bone case. Early 19th century.

sizes to fit the human form by Anatomical proportions in conjunction with geometrical Principles. The preface claimed its aim was "to promote a general knowledge of the science of cutting, which cannot be properly simplified without entering largely on the subject. All other works of the kind, published in Modern times, are so brief and mysterious that it is almost impossible for any person (if his intellects are ever so good) to gain but little information from them."

The following section gives such complex instructions and so many different aspects of the art that it is impossible not to feel sorry for the aspiring young tailor! Hearn strongly recommended the use of the "tape inch measure" as a tool of the trade, "it may appear difficult on the first inspection to those who have not been accustomed to the use of it, but I am persuaded, that if they would only take the trouble to practice two or three times, by measuring a coat, instead of the customer, and write the figures down, they would find it more expeditious, convenient, and correct, than the contemptible mode of using strips of parchment."

The adoption of the tape measure in the early 19th century was a significant step in that it helped to bring order and discipline to both tailoring and dressmaking. Without it, the detailed systems of cutting mens clothing that were to be developed throughout the 19th century would have been impossible.

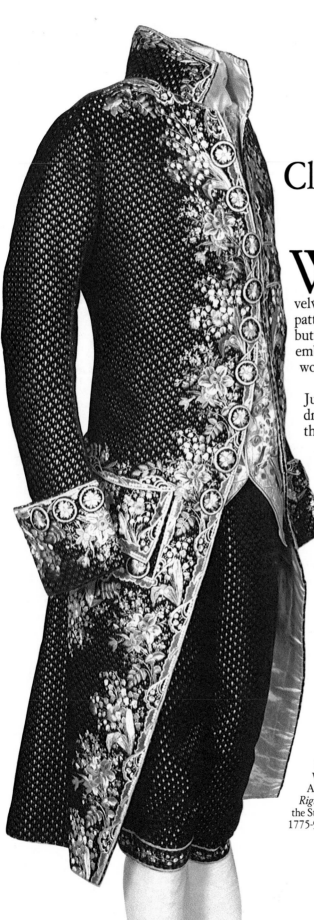

Clothes for the Occasion

While male everyday clothes were made increasingly of wool from the 1770s: for formal occasions such as court events, menswear became more and more decorative, with rich velvets and satins enhanced by exquisite embroidery in floral border patterns. Complementary designs were used on coat, waistcoat, buttons and knee breeches. This type of suit was probably embroidered before being cut out, either in English or French workshops.

Just as George III imposed conservative rules on female court dress resulting in wide hoops being worn under the armpits with the highwaisted neoclassical styles, so too, did male court dress assume a standard format in these years. Embroidered suits continued to be worn long after ordinary evening dress had become quite plain. It gradually became more stylised until, by the mid 19th century only a few sprigs on the waistcoat remained to tell of former glories.

These are two of six similar suits said to have been worn by Sir John Stanley of Alderley 1735-1807, Gentleman of the Privy Chamber to George III. Because the wearer was evidently very slim and fashion conscious, they may have been worn instead by his son, John Thomas Stanley, born in 1766, a well known writer and traveller, and Fellow of the Royal Society.

Court Suits Top Coat and Breeches in black silk velvet with purple satin figure in small diaper pattern. Waistcoat in ivory satin. All copiously embroidered with floral border pattern in pastel silks. British or French 1775-90. Worn by Lord Stanley of Alderley.
Right: Detail from another of the Stanley suits, deep blue velvet 1775-90.

Attributed to Nathaniel Dance *A Country Gentleman* (formerly called Dr. Charles Burney) c.1770 Oil on canvas 91.7 x 71.3 cms. unsigned. (Manchester City Art Galleries)

Richard Dighton.
Hand coloured engravings.
Left: A View from
Knightsbridge Barracks.
Capt. Horace Seymour. May 1817.
Right: Sir Francis Burdett
January 1820.

Cap^{tn} Horace Seymour

Drawn Etch^d   by Richard Dighton May 1817.

SIR FRANCIS BURDETT

The Old Great Coat

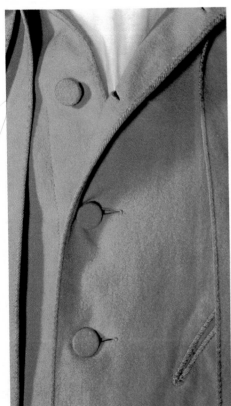

Above: Fawn cloth great coat with fawn velvet collar, and fawn twill silk ribbon bindings 1800-1825.

George Augustus Sala
Gaslight and Daylight 1859
Chapman and Hall

Things departed

"And, touching great-coats, are not great-coats themselves among the things departed? We have Paletôts, Ponchos, Burnouses . . . and a host of other garments, more or less answering the purpose of an overcoat.

But where is the great coat—the long, voluminous, wide-skirted garment of brown or drab broad cloth, reaching to the ankle, possessing unnumbered pockets; pockets for bottles, pockets for sandwiches, secret pockets for cash, and side-pockets for bank-notes? This venerable garment had a cape, which, in wet or snowy weather, when travelling outside the 'Highflyer' coach, you turned over your head. Your father wore it before you, and you hoped to leave it to your eldest sons. Solemn repairs—careful renovation of buttons and braiding were done to it, from time to time. A new great coat was an event—a thing to be remembered as happening once or so in a lifetime."

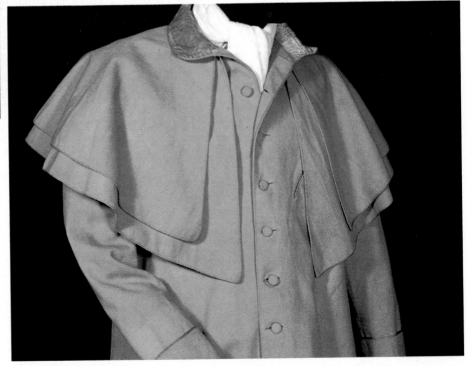

Sir Thomas Lawrence 1769—1830 *James Curtis 1750—1839, a London brewer c.1803.* Oil on canvas 128.7 x 102 x 7 cms. unsigned. (Manchester City Art Galleries)

The Tailor

English Trades
12th Edit. 1824 Sir Richard Phillips & Co. London.

"In a tailor's shop, where much business is carried on, there are always two divisions of workmen: first, the Foreman, who takes the measure of the person for whom the clothes are to be made, cuts out the cloth, and carries home the newly-finished garments to the customer; the others are mere working tailors who sit cross-legged on the bench, like the man near the window, represented in the plate; of these, very few know how to cut out, with any degree of skill, the clothes which they sew together.

The tools requisite in the business of a tailor are very few and inexpensive. The Sheers for the foreman, who stands to his work; for the others, a pair of scissors, a thimble, and needles of different sizes. In the thimble there is this peculiarity; that it is open at both ends. Besides these, there are required some long slips of parchment for measures, such as those represented against the wall, and an iron, called a goose, with this, when made hot, they press down the seams, which would otherwise take off from the beauty of the goods. The stand of the iron is generally a horseshoe, rendered bright from use. Before the foreman, as master, (for where the trade is not extensive the master cuts out, measures gentlemen, and carries home the clothes) is an open box; this contains buckram, tapes, bindings, trimmings, buttons etc., with which every master-tailor should be furnished, and from which they derive very large profits. On the shelf is a piece of cloth ready to be made into clothes, and also a pattern book.

… A writer on this subject says, that a master tailor ought to have a quick eye to steal the cut of a sleeve, the pattern of a flap, or the shape of a good trimming, at a glance; any bungler may cut out a shape when he has a pattern before him, but a good workman takes it by his eye in the passing of a chariot, or in the space between the door and a coach: he must be able not only to cut for the handsome and well-shaped, but bestow a good shape where nature has not granted it: he must make the clothes sit easy in spite of a stiff gait or awkward air: his hand and head must go together: he must be a nice cutter, and finish his work with elegance."

Tailor's Bill to Mr. Bury of Pendlehill. February 1816
Dr. to: Samuel Forster. Draper, Taylor and Ladies habit maker, Princes St. Corner of Clarence St. Manchester 4 Jan 1816.

4¼ Super Saxony black at 32/-		7.	4.6
Making Et Flannel linings	1.	5.	0
,, Breeches ,, ,,		14.	0
,, Waistcoat ,, ,,		11.	0
,, Leggings ,, ,,		7.	0
	£10.	1.	6.

The Tailor from *The Book of English Trades and Library of the Useful Arts.* Printed for Sir Richard Phillips & Co. 12th edition 1824.

Silhouette of an unknown woman 1820s.

Fine Linen

Fanny Jarvis: an unknown Englishwoman of the 1820s

Dr. Cunnington's collection includes a group of beautifully made underclothes, caps and linen marked "Fanny Jarvis," all dated between 1818 and 1836. Unfortunately he kept no record of the origins of his collection; perhaps the history of Fanny Jarvis was already lost. We can only guess that she was a typical gentlewoman of her day, blessed with ample means and fastidious taste, and that someone in her family thought her clothes worth preserving.

Night-dresses, a chemise, a morning gown, neck frills, a bustle, pockets and watch-pockets are all included in the collection. Sometimes, as with the caps, there are two or three identical specimens. All have been given a laundry number at the time of making. The night-dress is numbered 17, the chemise 9, and the highest number among the caps is 6. Though we do not know the contents of her complete linen closet, this suggests that Fanny Jarvis possessed at least a dozen and a half night-dresses and perhaps a dozen chemises. Her wardrobe also contained half a dozen each of plain striped white cotton nightcaps, finely checked white cotton nightcaps with "weepers" (long lappets), and white checked muslin morning caps with frills and embroidered insertions. The collection also includes two more elaborate morning caps of checked white cotton trimmed with East Midlands lace and puffs. These caps are marked "Fanny Jarvis Senr", and being in rather fussier taste they do indeed suggest an older woman. Even pre-Victorian manners enjoined simplicity and modesty on the young married woman.

We who throw our polyester/cotton undies into the washing machine cannot imagine how a dozen and a half night-dresses could possibly be necessary. We have probably been brought up to believe that our ancestors were far less scrupulous in their cleanliness than we are. By the early 1800's this was very far from the case. It is certain that Fanny Jarvis would have devoted infinitely more time and skill to the purchase, making, washing and care of her clothes than a modern woman.

The Bustle

No one can dispute that the introduction of this article was a decided improvement in the art of dress; giving, as it does, fulness and gracefulness to the figure, and causing the dress to sit easily and free from that straightness and angularity which is so completely destructive to the received notions of beauty—yet no article of dress has been more ridiculed.

Such treatment is, it must be confessed, not altogether undeserved, when we witness the monstrosities which under this name are occasionally adopted.

The bustle is an article the use of which requires the greatest circumspection. From its position, it is difficult for the wearer to be fully aware of its effect. Its amplitude ought, therefore, to be always regulated rather by the good taste of one on whom we can rely, than by our own feelings or predilections.

(The Art of Dress or Guide to the Toilette 1839.)

Underwear of 1825-35, showing Fanny Jarvis's cap, chemise, bustle (dated 1833) and pockets. The petticoat has a corded hem, edged with whitework embroidery. Down sleeve puffs are worn to support the "gigot" sleeve.

The Stages of the Toilette, unsigned lithographs, probably French c.1830.

Above: "Frills, Necklaces &c . . . If the neck is short, the greatest care must be taken to avoid everything which may tend to contract the distance between the head and the shoulders. A broad necklace, or a wide spreading collar, is certain destruction to a figure of this description. A very striking illustration of the bad effects of an ample collar on a short necked figure . . . is given in Plate V"
The Art of Dress 1839.

Left: Fanny Jarvis's double muslin ruffle, worn with a dress and pelerine of fawn silk, c.1824.
Right: Fanny Jarvis's single frill, marked "F.J.9," 40 inches (102 cm) long. Worn with a low-necked printed cotton dress, with Marino Faliéro sleeves, c.1835.

Opposite page.
"Do you please to have your bed warm'd Sir?"
Caricature of a housemaid by "Paul Pry" 1829. Note the creases in her sleeves showing the edge of her shoulder puffs.

Below:
Detail of the collar of the
morning gown, showing the
double puffing of muslin and the
muslin ruffle, which has to be
"got-up" with a goffering iron.

Bottom:
Morning gown marked "Fanny
Jarvis $\frac{1}{1823}$" and night cap marked
"Fanny Jarvis 3".

Laundry

Washing day in the nineteenth century was the most disruptive of all household rituals, involving much listing of linen, fetching and boiling of water, rubbing, scrubbing, rinsing and wringing. *The Workwoman's Guide* (1838) lists the equipment for a wash-house:-

Large and small washing tubs; a copper furnace in which to boil the linen (up to 18 or 20 gallons capacity for large washings); a maid or dolley (dollypeg for "possing" or agitating the clothes); worsted or flaxen washing lines; white wood line pegs; a rain water butt.

For the laundry one should have:-

Ironing cloths of flannel; a mangle; common irons for lighter articles; an Italian iron for frills (a type of goffering iron); a sleeve iron; a box iron; a gaufiering (sic) iron.

Goffering irons were used for the skilled task of getting up the numerous frills and ruffles on collars, caps and gentlemen's shirts.

The washing of plain whites was laborious enough:

"A good washer-woman will examine carefully the linen she has to wash, and rub soap onto such parts as require the most, as the collars and wristbands of shirts, taking care that the water is not too hot, otherwise it will set the dirt.

She afterwards twice thoroughly washes out all her white things in plenty of white warm lather, shaking each article out, and examining if every spot or stain is removed. She then boils them, taking care not to put too many in the copper at once.

A small quantity of soft soap thrown in to the boil helps to give a good colour to the linen, and if well washed out of the boil, as all linen ought to be, and afterwards well rinsed in plenty of spring water, no unpleasant smell will be retained.

The rinsing water should be made moderately blue by means of stone blue tied up in a flannel bag and squeezed in . . ."(*Workwoman's Guide*).

Large country houses had laundry-maids on the staff; according to Mark Girouard (*Life in the English Country House*) the young laundrymaids were often out in the yards fetching water and hanging washing, and their flirting with the grooms was a frequent breach of Victorian household discipline. Smaller households hired a washerwoman by the day, or brought in outside helpers to assist the womenfolk and domestics. A lady like Fanny Jarvis may have been able to afford to send washing out. Platt Hall appears to have had a laundry, but Mrs. Worsley, living at Platt Cottage, sent out washing to Mrs. Wellings of 5 Hardwick Street in 1868, and to both M. Bunting and E. Hughes in 1869. While Mrs. Worsley still lived at Platt Hall, she paid Hannah Mottershead to do the mangling, about twice a month regularly from 1857 to 1866, at a total yearly wage of about £2.10.0. to £2.15.0, depending on the size and frequency of washes. Washes sent out could be smaller; a typical bill of Mrs. Worsley consists of:

4 chemise	8d	1 pr cuffs	1d
2 drawers	4d	1 collar	1d
2 night gowns	6d	6 frills	3d
1 flannell	2d	1 Nt. cap	1d
4 stockings	4d	1 Habit-shirt	1d
18 pk handkerchiefs	9d		3.4

(Bill dated Dec. 1868, Platt Hall library).

LADY'S WASHING BOOK.

Number.		Price.	£.	s.
	Aprons	½		
	Caps, Bonnet	1		
	——— Night............................	1		
	Collars	1		
	Dresses	4d. or 6d.		
	Dressing Gowns.........................	3		
	Flannel ditto	3		
	Drawers	1		
	Flannel Petticoats	1		
	Flannel Drawers	2		
	Flannel Waistcoats	1		
	Frills	1		
	Habit Shirts	½		
	Jackets	2		
	Night Gowns	2		
	Neck Handkerchiefs	½		
	Pocket ditto	½		
	Napkins	½		
	Pockets	½		
	Petticoats	2		
	Socks, pairs of	1		
	Stockings, pairs of....................	1		
	Shifts	2		
	Stays	6		
	Skirts	2		
	Shawls	2		
	Tippets	1		

For most people, however, wash-day was at home, and even the best-regulated households regarded it with some dread. The tradition of wash-day Monday had a purpose—the left-over cold meat and pickles from Sunday dinner saved the added strain of cooking.

In Jane Austen's unfinished novel *The Watsons* (1804-5) Elizabeth Watson, eldest of a poor but genteel family, apologises for the lack of attention given to her sister Emma: "Since you have been at home, I have been so busy with my poor father and our great wash that I have had no leisure to tell you anything." Readers would have understood her dilemma at once.

It saved a great deal of time and effort to save up the dirty linen for infrequent great washes, rather than have frequent small ones. This explains the large numbers of undergarments and sheets thought necessary. *The Workwoman's Guide* says: "It is the best economy to wash by the year, or by the quarter, in places where it can be done, and by the score in preference to the piece."

The *Guide* gives a typical lady's washing book, suggesting "country prices" for each item. Note that it does not include such items as delicate lace. A lady like Fanny Jarvis would have supervised the cleaning of precious items herself, or would have entrusted them to her maid.

Altogether the *Workwoman's Guide* devotes twenty pages to recipes for stain removal, starching and goffering, including beer rinses to colour and stiffen lace. Lovers of Mrs Gaskell's *Cranford* will recall how pussy nearly choked on a saucer of milk containing an old and valuable lace collar. We do not recommend trying such methods on museum pieces!

Needlework

Fanny Jarvis's clothes are made of fine materials, sewn with tiny stitches and beautifully stroked gathers. It is likely that she made her caps and underlinen herself. They were certainly made in her household, and she would have supervised the purchase of materials, cutting out, sewing and marking.

> "Needlework is generally considered part of good housewifery.
> Many young women make almost everything they wear, by which they can make a respectable appearance at a small expense. Absolute idleness is inexcusable in a woman, and renders her contemptible. The needle is, or ought to be, always at hand for those intervals in which she cannot be otherwise employed".
>
> (*The Young Woman's Companion.* 1841).

Some ready-made caps, chemises etc. were on sale at this period, but it was more economical, and therefore more virtuous, for the middle-class housewife to make things by the batch at home. Mothers and daughters, wives and sisters set aside part of each day for such work, and made shirts, drawers and cravats for their menfolk as well. Jane Austen's letters are full of detail of her dressmaking and alterations. Even Jane Welsh Carlyle, who did not enjoy needlework, and used to repeat "being an only child I never wished to sew" until it became a family joke, made caps and gowns for herself, and a nightshirt for her husband, though his married sister was called on in 1842 to make him summer shirts and flannel winter shirts, presumably because they demanded greater skill.

Opposite page:
Woman Sewing, watercolour by William Henry Hunt (1790-1864) painted c.1830 (Manchester City Art Gallery).

Left:
Woman Sewing, a museum display at Platt Hall. The dress of white embroidered muslin dates from c.1830; the cap is marked "Fanny Jarvis 6." The workbox was a wedding present given to a Miss Pratt in 1835.

Patterns for caps, including "a young servant's neat day-cap" (fig 7 and 8) "a favourite cap for ladies and poor women" (fig 15, 16, 17, 18, 19) and "a neat comfortable day or night cap" (fig 20) Plate 9 from *The Workwoman's Guide* (1838).

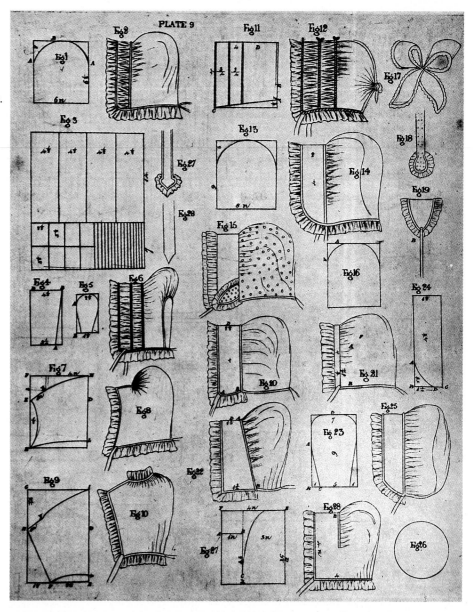

Books like *The Lady's Economical Assistant* by a Lady (1808) and *The Workwoman's Guide* by a Lady (1838) began to be published in the nineteenth century in response to a demand from the growing ranks of the middle class. They gave advice to "clergymen's wives, young married women, school-mistresses and ladies' maids" on cutting out and plain sewing, and became the forerunners of generations of household guides from Mrs. Beeton to the Superwoman books. Since these books were intended for lifelong reference, they sum up a tradition of domestic needlework, rather than promoting new fashions; the clothes illustrated are generally a little out of date. They make an interesting contrast to the ladies' magazines with their monthly fashion intelligence from Paris and London, and are much closer to the wardrobe of the average provincial woman.

Dresses may still be found in museums, which are cut from basic patterns in the style of a decade or two earlier than the dress, only the superficial ornament, the drapery of the skirt or the cut of the sleeve being changed with the times. We take this as a clue that the dress was home-made, or made by a small local dressmaker. Provincial women obviously clung to the techniques that they were taught.

Needlework and Charity

'Mrs. Norris began scolding: "That is a very foolish trick Fanny, to be idling away all the evening upon a sofa. Why cannot you come and sit here, and employ yourself as we do? — If you have no work of your own, I can supply you from the poor basket. There is all the new calico that was bought last week, not touched yet. I am sure I almost broke my back by cutting it out. You should learn to think of other people . . ."'.

(Jane Austen *Mansfield Park*, 1814).

Young women expected to spend part of their time sewing for the poor. Clergymen's wives often had charge of the parish box of child-bed linen for loan to poor women for the first month or so after the birth, and gifts, usually of infants' clothes, might be given to deserving families.

"I knew an amiable woman, who constantly kept a closet filled with articles of wearing apparel for the poor . . . It was also her custom to employ her children in the work; but it was always a mark of approbation for their good conduct, and it was considered a punishment when a child was denied the gratification of doing anything for her little neighbour. Thus the children acquired a taste for employment—a knowledge of needlework (which is, to all ranks of women, particularly useful), and an early habit of active benevolence."

(*The Lady's Economical Assistant,* 1808).

The anonymous author of the *Workwoman's Guide* hoped that the hints given in her book might eventually prove beneficial to the poor. She was probably thinking of the cottagers in rural parishes rather than of the urban and industrial working class. Her wish was fulfilled in part, for in 1850 her work is quoted as one of the sources for a new system of teaching needlework, *The Sampler* by a Lady.

From the early nineteenth century, plain needlework and knitting became an increasingly important part of the curriculum of the charity schools. It was considered one of the most important preparations for female adult life, for the wife and mother, for the domestic servant, and for the professional seamstress. Several groups, notably the National Society for Promoting the Education of the Poor in the Principles of the Established Church, published teaching manuals.

A group of dolls, representing a needlework class at a charity school c.1830-40

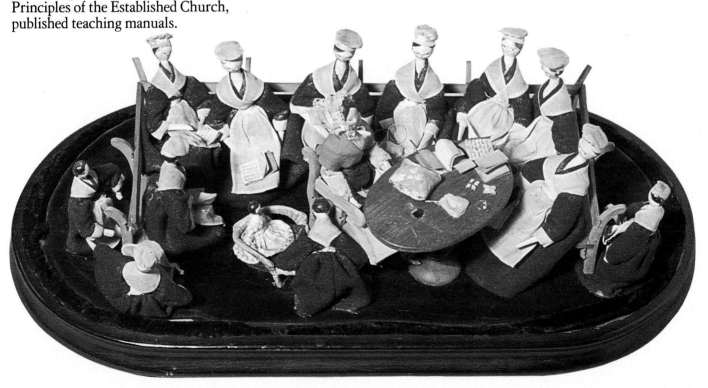

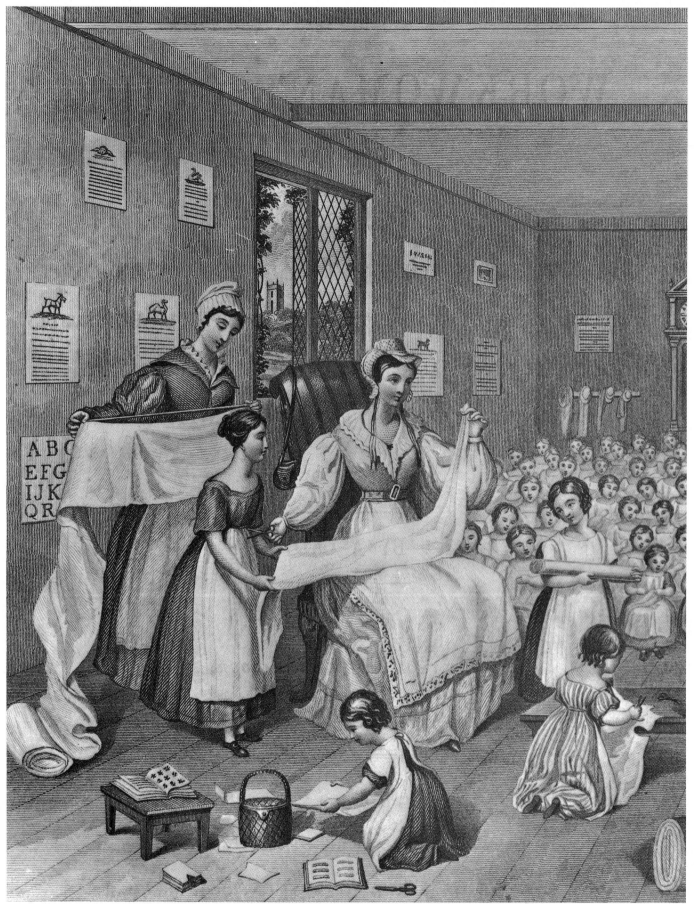

The frontispiece of *The Workwoman's Guide* by a Lady (1838) showing a sewing lesson at a village school, the older girls acting as teacher-assistants.

Children would be catechised on their method of work:

"Q. How do you hold your work?
A. Upon the forefinger of my left hand, and hold my finger straight before me.

Q. How do you hold your needle?
A. I turn the point towards me.

Q. Do you break off your cotton in your work?
A. No, I ask to have it cut off . . ."

(*The Sampler, or a System of Teaching Needlework in Schools* by a Lady, 1850).

Poor Jane Eyre must have gone through such an interview at Lowood School. Older girls who were proficient with their needles would be appointed teacher-assistants to the younger classes. Tickets would be given as rewards, and forfeits were given for losing or breaking a needle "or other misconduct". Unsaleable work made by the young ones would be cut up for patchwork, and a counterpane might be made as the grand prize for the most deserving girl.

Many charitable ladies interested themselves in the promotion of needlework teaching in schools. Certain specialist industries were founded or revived in order to relieve distress. The Irish lace and crochet industries, for example, were organised and promoted commercially in response to the Great Hunger of 1847, and a fashion for Irish products was created. The motives of these ladies were of the highest, and their influence pervades education to this day. Many readers will have been taught to sew by producing a book of sample buttonholes and seams.

Nevertheless, the stress laid on the virtue and importance of the needle may have been a mixed blessing. We may get great pleasure from contemplating the beautiful work of Fanny Jarvis, done in moments of quiet industry.
But for every lady like her, there was a young woman trying to make a respectable life for herself in an over-stocked labour market, her skill with the needle her only asset.

No one who has not been a frequent visitor in the homes of the poor, is aware of the extravagance and waste usual among women of a humble class, arising from their total ignorance of matters of cutting out and needlework . . . The same ignorance and unskilfulness, and the same consequent waste of laborious and scanty earnings is common among our female household servants: who by putting out their clothes to dressmakers pay nearly half as much for the making up as for the materials. The direct saving of expense upon articles of dress, were they qualified to work for themselves, would be an important annual item. But the indirect and further benefit would be of infinitely more account. The thrifty disposition, the regularity and neatness, the ideas of order and management, inspired by the conscious ability and successful exertion, in one leading branch of good housewifery, cannot be too highly prized or diligently cultivated, for the result is *moral*. The orderly house but reflects the orderly mind . . ."

(Introduction from *The Workwoman's Guide 1838* by a Lady.)

Dressmaking and Millinery

English Trades 1824—The Ladies' Dress-Maker

"Measuring the Chest" from
*The Manual of Needlework for
the Use of National Schools*
Commissioners of National
Education Ireland 1873.

"Under this heading we shall include not only the business of a Mantua-maker, but also of a Milliner: for, although in London these two parts of in fact the same trade, are frequently separate, they are not always so, and in the country they are very commonly united . . .

In the Milliner, taste and fancy are required; with a quickness in discerning, imitating, and improving upon various fashions, which are perpetually changing among the higher circles.

. . . the Ladies' Dress-Maker's customers are not always easily pleased; they frequently expect more from their dress than it is capable of giving . . .

. . . The Dress-Maker must be an expert anatomist; and must, if judiciously chosen, have a name of French termination; she must know how to hide all defects in the proportions of the body, and must be able to mould the shape by the stays, that, while she corrects the body, she may not interfere with the pleasures of the palate.

The business of a Ladies' Dress-Maker and Milliner, when conducted upon a large scale and in a fashionable situation, is very profitable; but the mere work-women do not get anything at all adequate to their labour.
They are frequently obliged to sit up very late, and the recompense for the extra work is, in general, a poor remuneration for the time spent.
The plate represents the Dress-Maker taking the pattern off from a lady, by means of a piece of paper or cloth: the pattern, if taken in cloth, becomes afterwards the lining of the dress." From the *Book of English Trades and Library of Useful Arts* Sir Richard Phillips & Co. 12th Edition, 1824.

The term "Mantua-maker" went back to the late 17th century when that garment was fashionable. It was still used in the 19th century to denote a lady's dressmaker, long after mantuas had ceased to be worn.
Milliners traditionally sold haberdashery and trimmings—goods which originally came from Milan. By the late 18th century, they also made the dresses and hats which the trimmings went on. It was only by the end of the 19th century that the milliner exclusively made or sold hats.
While some dresses were always made at home, most classes of society traditionally had their dresses made professionally. Particularly in the 19th century there were a large number of dressmakers available, this being one of the few areas open to the many women forced to support themselves.
Moreover, paper patterns and sewing machines did not come into general use until after 1860, and even the tape-measure was a rarity in the early 19th century. Women's garments fitted more closely than they do today, and it was

The Ladies Dressmaker from *The Book of English Trades and Library of Useful Arts.* Printed for Sir Richard Phillips and Co. 12th Edition 1824.

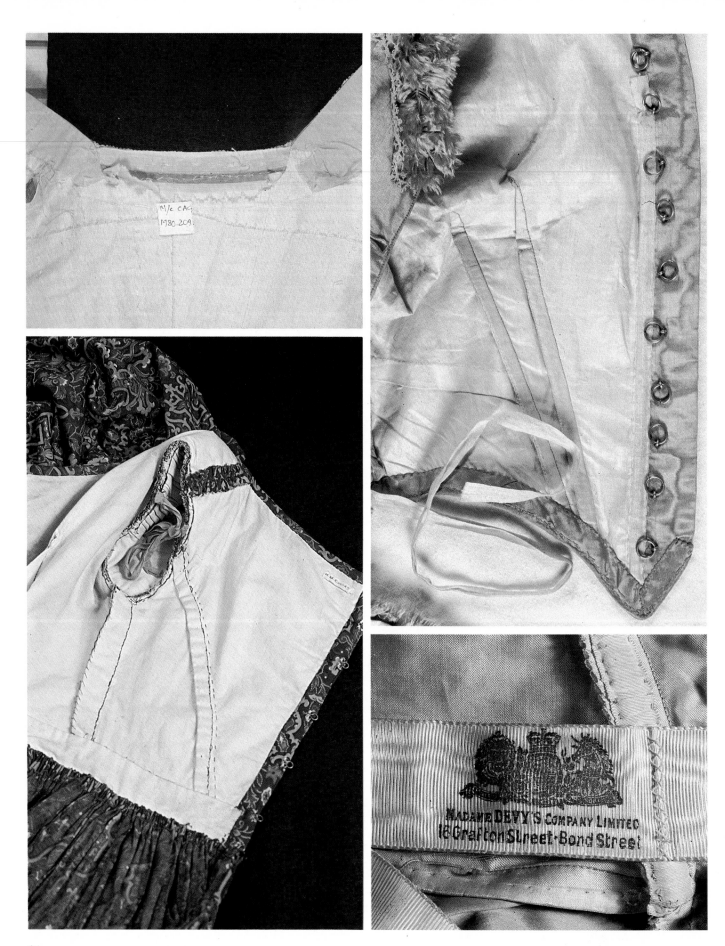

Top left: Yellow green and red striped silk dress c.1775 showing interior of back bodice, with typical rough stitching of late 18th century.
Top right: Light blue moiré silk wedding dress 1865, showing glazed cotton lining, extensive boning and machine stitching. The bust is padded inside the lining.
Below left: Dark red printed dress c.1837 showing stout cotton lining.
Below right: Waistband label from evening dress in beige satin. 1873-75.

difficult for the amateur to achieve satisfactory results. Because of this, *The Workwoman's Guide* (1838) stated in its section on home dress-making "it is strongly recommended to all those who can afford it, to have their best dresses invariably made by a mantua-maker, as those which are cut out at home, seldom fit so comfortably, or look so well, as when made by persons in constant practice".

Other books recommended unpicking an old professionally made bodice and using it as a guide by which to cut out new garments. A woman might choose material from the dressmaker's stock, but she would often buy her own, with trimmings, from a draper, or travelling "Manchester Man", and give it to the dressmaker who returned the completed dress, preferably with a bundle of surplus material which could be used later. Dresses were frequently remodelled, and, if of silk, perhaps "turned", to expose the underside fabric. For this reason, silk skirts were always lined to preserve their freshness. All bodices were lined with a stout fabric, usually cotton or linen. As described in the passage above, this was cut out first to give the right dimensions and shape, so that the expensive fabric might not be wasted by being cut wrongly. After the briefest measurements were taken with a piece of ordinary tape, the lining was cut against the body, and the main fabric cut by it. In the early part of the century, the front was cut on the bias, and decorations could be draped or pleated over the flat lining. These were jobs for the most skilled assistants in the shop. The younger apprentices would stitch the skirts, leaving slits to reach the hanging pockets beneath, and prepare the piping which strengthened and decorated many of the bodice seams. They would also run errands to match fabrics and trimmings at different shops, and, of course, pick up the pins.

Fitting skirt to bodice was a skilled job; gathers had to be stroked into place, or pleats arranged. The fine "gauging" at the back—a type of cartridge pleating used to give a good "tournure"—had to be set in exactly the right position. The skirt top and lining would be turned under together, following the line of the bodice as it was worn, often in a deep "V", and the two edges oversewn together; the extra fabric was left in place since it gave the skirts a nice "lift". Variety was provided in the shape of the sleeves and neckline, and by superficial decorations. Finally the bodice would usually be fastened at the back with large flattened brass hooks and eyes. All the seams were neatened by oversewing, and by the late 1830s, split whale bones were beginning to be sewn onto them in casings. These were to be more extensively used as the century progressed, and were considered essential to give the correct shape to the dress, as the plate shows. They would have been worn in addition to a tightly laced corset.

Lock stitch sewing machine c.1868
Made by Bradbury and Company Wellington Works,
Oldham.
White cotton dress printed with purple stripes
1860-65.
White cotton broderie anglaise cap 1860-65.

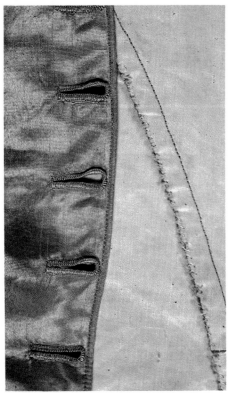

Detail of lockstitch machine stitching from 1865
wedding dress on previous page.

This illustration shows machine stitching. The sewing machine was perfected by Elias Howe in 1846 in America, but made commercially viable by Isaac Meritt Singer who patented his lock-stitch machine in 1852 and opened an agency to sell it in Glasgow in 1856. It was not until 1860, when the English patent on Howe's original machine expired, that Singer and other firms were free to market the sewing machine throughout Britain. It was anticipated that this would make dressmaking easier: in fact, the time saved in sewing was gradually taken up as the machine was used to create more and more elaborate trimmings. By the 1870s, the simple lines of the early Victorian dress were gone for ever—lost under a mass of flounces and ruches.

When a lady decided to have a dress made, she would first get an idea of styles from fashion plates in magazines, and from her friends' clothes.
The dressmaker might then call at her home, or the lady would go to the dressmaker's establishment, where she might be shown model dresses worn by the prettiest apprentice, and be assisted in making her choice. This was not always easy. Mrs. Merrifield, in *Dress as a Fine Art* (1854) described what happened:

"Instead of the beautiful, the graceful, the becoming, what are the attractions offered by the dressmakers? What are the terms used to invite the notice of customers? Novelty and distinction; the shops are "Magasins de Nouveautés", the goods are "distingués", "recherchés", "nouveaux", "the last fashion", the new fashions are exhibited on the elegant person of one of the dressmaker's assistants, who is selected for this purpose, and are adopted by the purchaser without reflecting how much of the attraction of the dress is to be ascribed to the fine figure of the wearer, how much to the beauty of the dress, or whether it will look equally well on herself.
So the fashion is set, and then it is followed by others, until at last it becomes singular not to adopt some modification of it, although the extreme may be avoided."

The good dressmaker might, however, guide the wearer towards a suitable dress, perhaps with the aid of Mrs. Merrifield's book, or the many others like it, which set out rules for "correct" dress. Great care had to be taken in dressing to complement the complexion:
"Skyblue is always considered as most becoming to fair persons, and it contrasts more agreeably than any other colour with the complementary orange, which constitutes the key-note, as it were, of the general hue of the complexions and hair of this type . . .

Newest Fashions for May 1829
Morning & Evening Dresses.

W. Alais Sc.

"Newest Fashions for May 1829 Morning and Evening Dresses" *World of Fashion* Hand coloured engraving.

Draperies of a dead white, like cambric muslin, are becoming to fresh complexions, the rosy tints of which they vivify, but they do not suit thick and unpleasant complexions."

Some dressmakers became extremely rich. Jane Clarke, with a fashionable London clientele, left £80,000 when she died in 1859 and, it is said, requested to be buried in her point lace. At the other end of the scale was the small Manchester concern where Mrs. Gaskell's Mary Barton became an apprentice, belonging to "a certain Miss Simmonds, milliner and dressmaker, in a respectable little street leading off Ardwick Green, where her business was duly announced in gold letters on a black ground, enclosed in a bird's eye maple frame, and stuck in the front parlour window, where the workwomen were called "her young ladies" and where Mary was to work for two years without any rumuneration, on consideration of being taught the business; and where afterwards she was to dine and have tea, with a small quarterly salary (paid quarterly because so much more genteel than by the week) a very small one, divisible into a minute weekly pittance. In summer she was to be there by six, bringing her day's meals during the first two years: in winter she was not to come in till after breakfast. Her time for returning home at night must always depend upon the quantity of work Miss Simmonds had to do".

Mary's lateness in walking home at night was to bring her to the attentions of Henry Carson, a mill owner's son, who tried to seduce her. This was a well-known problem for these young women, made more acute by the fact that, while being very poor, they were often inclined to be interested in pretty clothes, and easily fell prey to such men as Carson. In slack seasons, as in the summer, some were known to supplement their income by prostitution.

Mrs. Gaskell wrote *Mary Barton* in 1848, at the end of a decade in which public concern for the plight of the dressmaker had reached a high pitch. Awareness of their working conditions had been heightened by the publication in 1843 of the report of the Parliamentary Commission into the employment of children and young persons. This heard that in the busy season it was common to work 18 hours a day. One of the worst cases described was of a girl "compelled to remain without changing her dress for nine days and nights successively. During this period, she had been permitted only occasionally to rest on a mattress placed on the floor, for an hour or two at a time, and her meals were placed at her side cut up, so that as little time as possible should be spent in their consumption. This girl, 17 years of age, had totally lost her sight from continued labour."

This extract was from the report of R. D. Grainger, who went on to state, "the protracted labour described above is, I believe, quite unparalleled in the history of manufacturing processes. I have looked over a considerable proportion of the report of the factory commission, and there is nothing in the accounts of the worst conducted factories to be compared with the facts elicited in the present inquiry".

Many writers used the material given in this report, which dealt with all kinds of needlewomen, from dressmakers to those working in the wholesale clothing trades as a basis for plays, books and novels. Today, none are better known than the articles and cartoons published in "Punch", which included Hood's *Song of the Shirt.*

Gent pursuing milliner from Albert Smith *The Natural History of the Gent* 1847.

With fingers weary and worn,
    With eyelids heavy and red,
A Woman sat, in unwomanly rags,
    Plying her needle and thread—
Stitch! stitch! stitch!
    In poverty, hunger, and dirt,
And still with a voice of dolorous pitch
She sang the 'Song of the Shirt!'

• • • •

'Work—work—work
    Till the brain begins to swim,
Work—work—work
    Till the eyes are heavy and dim!
Seam, and gusset, and band,
    Band, and gusset, and seam,
Till over the buttons I fall asleep
    And sew them on in a dream!

'O, Men with Sisters dear!
    O Men! with Mothers and Wives!
It is not linen you're wearing out,
    But human cretures' lives!
    Stitch—stitch—stitch,
    In poverty, hunger, and dirt,
Sewing at once, with a double thread,
    A Shroud as well as a Shirt.

'But why do I talk of Death?
    That Phantom of grisly bone,
I hardly fear his terrible shape,
    It seems so like my own—
It seems so like my own,
    Because of the fasts I keep;
O God! that bread should be so dear,
    And flesh and blood so cheap!

• • • •

'Seam, and gusset, and band,
    Band, and gusset, and seam,
Work, work, work,
    Like the Engine that works by Steam!
A mere machine of iron and wood
    That toils for Mammon's sake—
Without a brain to ponder and craze,
    Or a heart to feel—and break!"

From Thomas Hood,
    The Song of the Shirt, 1843

Milliner's wooden delivery box 1820-50 inscribed
"H. W. Friend Milliner etc.".
Dummy head for making caps 1830-60, papier
mâché and plaster of Paris.
Wedding bonnet, cream silk with cream crêpe
trimming and artificial lilacs 1835-39.

Love & Marriage

c.1840

"The great end and aim of almost every young female is to be united in marriage to a deserving man" *The Young Lady's book of advice and instruction* 1859.

By the opening of Queen Victoria's reign, woman's rôle was widely defined as being the helpmate of man and mother of his children. Without marriage, her mission in life could never be fulfilled. Moreover, while the spinster could always be found work around the family home in the country, in the newly developing town life, there was no place for the unmarried daughter, who found the very few opportunities for employment, such as dressmaking, were poorly paid. Therefore, husbands equalled meal tickets.

This was an age when great reliance was placed on inherited wealth. Prospective husbands were advised to choose, if not a bride with a generous "settlement" from her family, then at least one who would take care of the family fortune, and not fritter it away. An etiquette book in Platt Hall's library from around 1850 warns—

"Love as natural to youth as hunger or thirst, and so fascinating in its influence over the mind and feelings, that not unfrequently, every other thought, wish, and care, is absorbed in this one great passion, thus it is, that many early imprudent marriages are daily contracted, a fatal and irretrievable error . . . Whatever may be the personal attractions of a female, if she does not possess the superior ones of religion, industry and chastity, it is impossible that she can become a good wife."

Etiquette for ladies and gentlemen, or the Principles of True Politeness c.1850

Albert Smith *The Flirt* 1848.

In addition to any financial endowment, a bride also came to her husband's family provided with enough clothing, particularly underwear, to last her for years to come. Her trousseau would often be proudly displayed to friends and visitors: Lady Dorothy Neville recalled seeing that of Lady Sarah Villiers, who married Prince Nicholas Esterhazy in 1842.

"I perfectly remember her magnificent trousseau, the piles of lovely things, and above all, the ornamental lace and flower tops to the long gloves, of which there were dozens and dozens, as it were provision for a lifetime. In those days, people laid in an enormous stock when they were married, and stored up things which now would be discarded or given away." (Lady Dorothy Neville *Reminiscences*. 1906.)

For more ordinary girls, the preparations for marriage would involve weeks spent hand hemming delicate handkerchiefs, chemises and bed-linen for their

Wedding accessories from the mid 19th century.

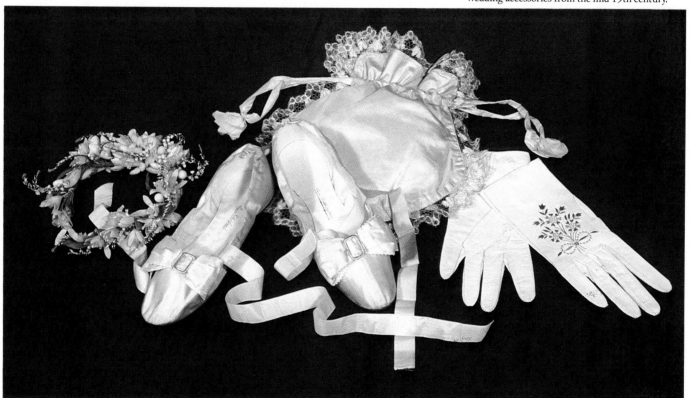

bottom drawer. Rosamond Vincy in George Eliot's *Middlemarch* enlisted the help of Mary Garth and a Miss Morgan to stitch her trousseau. Although her prospective husband was not well-off, she insisted on the highest quality; all her cambric frilling was to be double hemmed and beyond the necessary half dozen "first rate pocket handkerchiefs" Rosamond "contented herself without the very highest style of embroidery and Valenciennes".

Even the wedding dress was looked upon as an investment for the future. Today's impractical creations in white nylon and machine lace, worn once, then stored forever, would have astounded the Victorian bride.
Her dress varied only slightly from ordinary fashions. Its colour was not white, but instead pale blue, dove grey or fawn silk. She would have worn it as best for as long as she could after marriage, perhaps until she was expecting her first child. Then she too, like the modern bride, often stored it away as a treasured souvenir.

Because of this custom, wedding dresses are perhaps one of the types of garment most frequently offered to museums from the Victorian period. The costume collection at Platt Hall includes over a hundred examples. Wedding dresses are one of the rare types of garment for which the name of the wearer and the date of her marriage are often recorded. Few other garments come to us with so much information.

In 1839 Elizabeth Priestman could not have known that the man she was marrying, John Bright of Rochdale, was to become nationally famous in the next decade, as a radical politician and champion of free trade. The Brights were Quakers, like many early reformers, and would have been married quietly in a Friends' Meeting House, with little ceremony. Since the 18th century, Quaker women had worn a distinctive plain costume, which expressed their denial of worldly vanity through its absence of pattern, bright colour or elaborate trimming.

While particularly the older Quaker women's dresses were based on styles prevalent many years previously, Elizabeth's dress follows the current fashionable outline with its full sleeves, held in at the upper arm, pleated bodice and pelerine or cape. Perhaps because Quakers scorned the ephemeral, their surviving garments, such as this dress, are usually of a very high quality, both of fabric and workmanship. It is possible, that her characteristic stiff brimmed Quaker bonnet and starched muslin cap may not have been worn for the wedding, but were made slightly later since the low crown is more typical of the early 1840s.

As a complete contrast, the wedding dress on the left is highly ornamented. On a densely patterned jacquard woven silk brocade in blue and white are superimposed scallops of cobweb-like blonde lace in cream silk.
This lace was popular throughout the early 19th century; it could be easily made on newly invented machines, yet its fragility made it a luxury.
It is a miracle that so much has survived on this dress: in many places it is in tatters. The bonnet and veil dating from 1835-9 were probably also worn for weddings. The dress was worn and the reticule carried by Anne Payne on April 13th 1839 when she married Thomas Field, a member of a prosperous farming family in Wallingford, Berkshire. Anne was only 21 when she married. She was to bear eight sons and three daughters, and die in 1859 at the age of 41. This waistcoat belonged to Anne's husband and was probably worn by him on his wedding day in 1839. Light patterned waistcoats were commonly worn on such occasions, and they too were often preserved by their wearers.

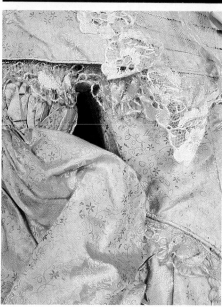

It would be nice to think that Mr. Field, like Mr. Robinson, who married Miss Willis, "a gentleman in public service, with a good salary and a little property of his own besides" described by Dickens in *Sketches by Boz* (1837) wore with his waistcoat "a light blue coat and double milled kersey pantaloons, white neckerchief, pumps and dress gloves." For the occasion, the Willis's cook wore "a large white bow of unusual dimensions, in a much smarter headdress than the regulation cap". It was common practice for such bridal favours to be distributed among household servants, and for more elaborate ones to be given to the wedding guests.

In *The Workwoman's Guide* (1838) bridal favours are discussed: "Sometimes white ribbons, gloves and handkerchiefs are given, and sometimes only the former. Favours for the higher orders are usually of lace, flowers, silver ribbon, or cord, and those for the middling classes, of satin ribbon. They are worn on the left side, the usual quantity given to servants, both men and women, coachmen etc. is three yards, which is

worn as a trimming for either the cap or bonnet by the women, and made up into very large bows for the men, to pin on their coats".
The custom survives today in the sprays of carnations worn by principal wedding guests.

At this time, the practice of bride and bridesmaids wearing flowers and carrying bouquets was becoming common, orange blossom especially being favoured.

Fashion plate from
*Townsend's Monthly Magazine
of Parisian Fashions* c.1850.
Hand coloured engraving.

Below: Detail of embroidery on
dress.

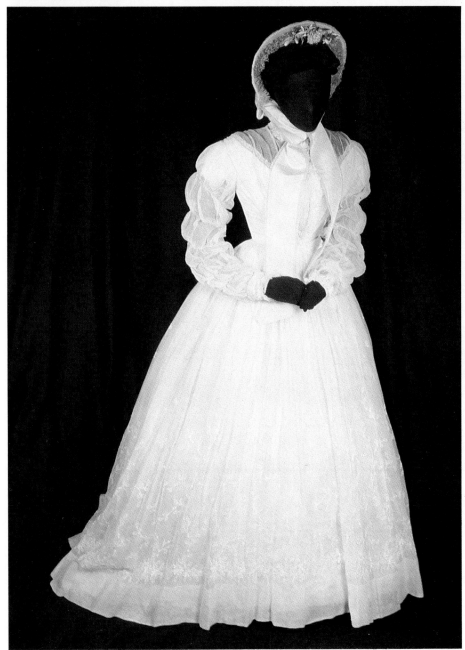

Left: White cotton gauze dress
with "tambour work"
embroidery (chain stitch worked
with a fine hook). Worn by
Elizabeth Anna Burrow, born
17 May 1837, at her wedding on
1st October 1864 to Franke
Freeman Parker, a clerk, at
Southampton.
Bonnet—white crêpe decorated
with artificial orange blossoms
and camellias and white silk
ribbon. Worn by Elizabeth
Goodier on her marriage to
Abraham Haworth in Eccles
Congregational Church
5th September 1861. This came
to the Museum in a wooden box
labelled "My Wedding Bonnet
with veil removed".

Marriage in High Life: *Gavarni in London*

"At St. George's Church, Hanover Square, by the Right Reverend the Bishop of London, the Right Honourable the Earl of Normandale, eldest son of the Marquis of Hallidon, K.G., to Katherine, second daughter of John, Earl of Dashmore. The lovely bride, who wore a splendid dress of entirely British manufacture, was accompanied to the altar by a numerous circle of relations, and given away by her noble father.
At the conclusion of the ceremony the happy pair started in a carriage and four for Dodsworth Park, the seat of the Duke of Thanet, uncle to the bride, where they intend to pass the honeymoon.
"An elegant déjeuner was given by the Countess of Dashmore at her mansion in Berkeley Square, to the relatives of the newly-married couple, and to some of the élite of the nobility, among whom were the Duke and Duchess of ...., the Marquis of ...., the Earls of ...., and, &c., &c., &c."

Often may paragraphs similar to the above be read, chiefly towards the end of the season, in the fashionable journals of our metropolis, with, in general, many additional observations by the penny-a-liners of the day, as how the beauteous bride was overcome by her feelings, and how she was related to this and that illustrious personage; all which is greedily read and regarded as most important information by the inhabitants of the three kingdoms, while many a country Miss envies the happiness of Lady Katherine, making conjectures as to whether she be dark or fair, and whether she has plenty of jewels; and thinks how delightful it is to be a Countess.

All this is the bright side of the picture. Were there no dark side, fashionable weddings would be scenes from the garden of Eden, or tableaux from Paradise (not a Mahometan one). All, however, is not gold that glitters, and could we see through the blonde and silk that covers the bosom of the fair bride, and obtain a view of the heart beneath, we should probably be let into the secret of many sad sacrifices made to the Mammon of wealth and rank.

It may be imagined, that Lady Katherine Dashmore could not possibly be incommoded by any of those faults which emanate from the heart. Surely such a one could never be so foolish as to fall in love with anything but a title and a large estate . . . Still, notwithstanding all the maternal precepts that had been instilled into her mind, Lady Katherine was actually foolish enough to fall in love with a younger brother.

. . . The contraband love affair between Lady Katherine and Augustus Courtenay must, however, have been discovered by the eagle eyes of Lady Dashmore; and it may be perceived how successfully she has opposed its progress, on reading the paragraph containing the account of her daughter's marriage with Lord Normandale—a young nobleman noted for imbecility and ugliness, and whose mind is as narrow as his chest. Look, however, at his "happy" bride as she approaches the altar. Do not imagine that she is at all downcast, because her face wears an expression of sadness. Oh no! that cannot of course arise from her observing that Augustus Courtenay is gazing upon the ceremony from a distant corner, but from the emotion naturally caused by leaving her family; and that flood of tears into which she bursts as she enters the carriage, followed by her noble and wealthy husband, has probably the same origin, and not from any comparison between the rejected and the accepted crossing her mind.

"Marriage in High Life" from *Gavarni in London: Sketches of Life and Character* Edited by Albert Smith 1849.

The Gent

What was a "Gent"? Whatever else he might be he was most definitely not a "gentleman"—according to the chroniclers of early Victorian society, who were beginning to note the emergence of this species in their city streets and pleasure grounds. One writer, Albert Smith, gave his opinion of this new phenomenon in *The Natural History of the Gent,* published in 1847.

"Our attention was first called to Gents in the following manner: We were in the habit of occasionally coming into contact with certain individuals, who when they spoke of their acquaintances were accustomed to say "I know a gent", or, "A gent told me". Never by any good luck did we hear them speak of Gentlemen. But it occurred that we chanced, on future occasions, to see one or two of the Gents above alluded to, and then we understood what they were . . .

The first Gent we ever saw, we encountered on the roof of an omnibus, with his hat a little on one side, and a staring shawl round his neck. He was also smoking a cigar, as he sat next to the driver . . .

We met the next Gent in the boxes at one of the theatres, whither he had come in a full-dress of a light blue stock, and cleaned white gloves re-dirtied. We knew they had been cleaned; they exhaled a faint camphine odour, as he put his hand on the brass rail and leant over us, and there was none of that sharpness of outline in their dirt, which new gloves evince: it was denser, cloudier, more universal; and the knuckles and nails were remarkably so. This Gent also had a little stick. He lighted a cigar at the lobby-lamp on leaving the house, and pulled a staring shawl out of his hat as he whistled an air from one of the burlesques". . .

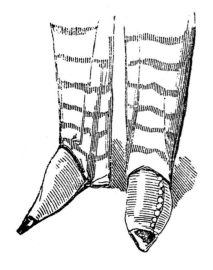

"The finest specimens may be seen in the coloured "Fashions", with which certain comically-disposed tailors adorn their windows. In these presumed representations of prevalent style, some favourite west-end locality is taken for the background; and, in front, are many Gents, in such attitudes, as may display their figures and little boots to the best advantage.
Some are supposed to be arrayed for an evening party, in green dress coats and puce tights. Some again, are represented as sportsmen, with pinched-in waists, that the shock of the first leap, or the kick of the first shot, would knock in half; and others are promenade Gents, in frock coats and corded trousers, bowing to one another with much grace, or leading little Gents by the hand, who look like animated daguerreotypes of themselves. Well, then, these are Gents, "pur sang". Observe, as the showman says, observe their fashionably-shaped hats, their Lilliputian boots, their tiny gloves . . .

All on this page and overleaf
right taken from Albert Smith:
*The Natural History of the
Gent* 1847.

One has only to look into the advertisements of cheap tailors, and the
windows of ticketed shops, to form a very good notion of the other
principal marks by which the Gent may be distinguished.
. . . To his taste does the ready-made Shoemaker appeal in the short fancy
"Alberts", ticketed "The fashion" . . . The most favourite style of
"chaussure" is a species of cloth-boot, with a shiny leather toe, and a close
row of mother-of-pearl shirt-buttons down the front; not for any purpose,
for they are simply sewn on, the real method of fastening on the brodequin
being by the humble lace and tag of domestic life, at the side.
But it is with the Haberdashers that the toilet of the Gents comes out
strongest. You will see "Gent's Dress Kid" ticketed in the window.
Be sure that these are large-sized, awkwardly cut, yellow kid gloves,
at one and sixpence . . .

. . . And then the stocks—what marvellous cravats they form!
Blue always the favourite colour—blue, with gold sprigs! blue,
with crimson floss-silk flower! blue Joinvilles, with rainbow ends!
And, if they are black and long, they are fashioned into quaint
conceits: frills of black satin down the front, or bands of the
same fabric looking like an imitation of crimped skate; or
studs of jet made like buttons, as if Gent wore a cheap, black
satin shirt, and that was where it fastened . . .

. . . And they love rings in profusion, which we have seen them
at times wear outside their gloves. But this, perhaps, was an
advantage, as gents are accustomed, in general, to wear their
hands large and red, with flattened ends to the fingers."

Herein lay Smith's main objection to the Gent. The real gentleman should have snowy white hands with elegant fingers untainted by work. An etiquette book for this period pointed out:

"It is not to be imagined that richness of clothing or a display of jewellery constitutes a person's being well dressed. It is of very little consequence what style of dress you wear in the street, providing it fits you well and be in good taste. I need hardly remark that a gentleman never wears shabby gloves or a bad hat, nor will he ever be seen in the drawing room in a surtout. Cleanliness is a prominent feature in the appearance of a gentleman . . . a disregard of cleanliness is a direct insult to society, and is a certain indication of filthy habits and a vulgar education."
Etiquette for Ladies & Gentlemen c.1850

Any deviation from this ideal would suggest a plebian rather than a patrician background. To Smith and many others, the Gent was an upstart from the lower orders, trying through mistakenly showy clothes, and an affected manner, to rise above his God-given station:

"Their strenuous attempts to ape gentility are to us more painful than ludicrous. And the labouring man, dressed in the usual costume of his class is, in our eyes, far more respectable than the gent, in his dreary efforts to assume a style and tournure which he is so utterly incapable of carrying out."

Such protestations as this were futile. The Gent was a product of the modern world. He earned his living in shops and offices, warehouses and counting houses. He was one of the new breed of wage earners, whose small salaries were yet sufficient to provide some luxuries in life, and whose education, though basic, encouraged him to dream of rising beyond his humble position. Smith was right to see him as a threat to the established order. Modern trade needed the Gent, and others like him, to work for it and to buy its products. So the Gent continued to flourish and does so to this day.

Charles Dickens, himself often described as a "Gent" rather than a gentleman because of his flashy style of dress, has provided us with many fascinating descriptions of Gents, showing how they could be found in every stratum of society where men had aspirations, such as Mr. Dowler's friend, immortalised in the *Posthumous Papers of the Pickwick Club:*

"A charming young man of not much more than fifty, dressed in a very bright blue coat with resplendent buttons, black trousers, and the thinnest possible pair of highly polished boots. A gold eye glass was suspended from his neck by a short broad black ribbon, a gold snuff box was lightly clasped in his left hand; gold rings innumerable glittered on his fingers and a large diamond pin set in gold glistened in his shirt frill. He had a gold watch, with a gold curb chain with large gold seals and he carried a pliant ebony cane with a heavy gold top. His linen was of the very whitest, finest and stiffest, his wig of the glossiest, blackest and curliest. His snuff was prince's mixture: his scent "Bouquet du Roi". His features were contracted into a perpetual smile; and his teeth were in such perfect order that it was a difficult task at a small distance to tell the real from the false."

Fashion Plate "Gentleman's Fashions for October 1830, Shooting, Morning and Riding Dresses" Hand coloured engraving.

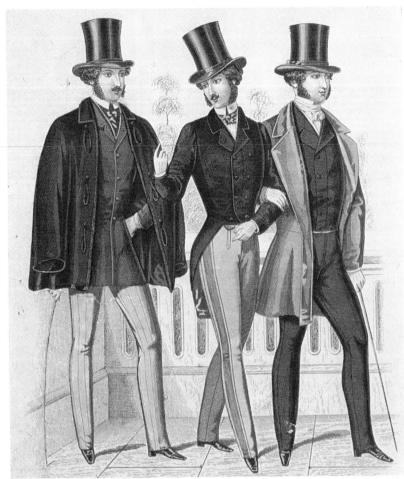

Hand coloured engravings.

Right: Fashion Plate from *The Gentleman's Magazine* October 1851.

Below: Fashion Plate "Winter Fashions for 1845."

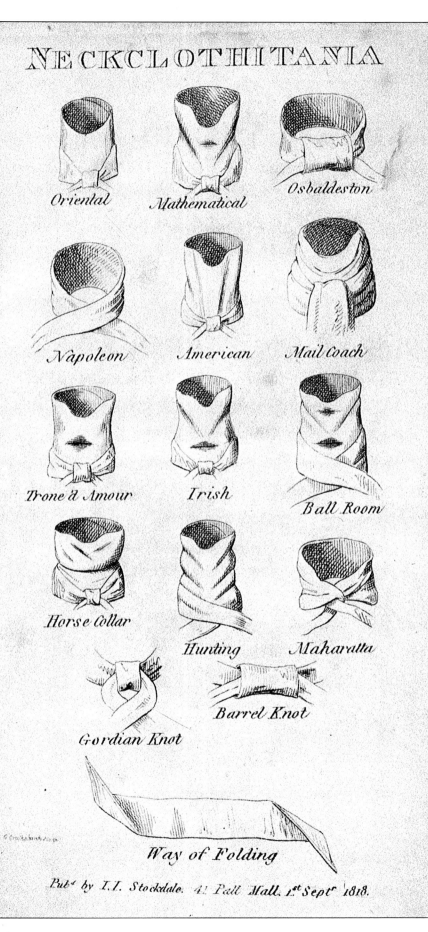

NECKCLOTHITANIA

Oriental   Mathematical   Osbaldeston

Napoleon   American   Mail Coach

Trone d'Amour   Irish   Ball Room

Horse Collar   Hunting   Maharatta

Gordian Knot   Barrel Knot

Way of Folding

Pubd by I.I. Stockdale. 41 Pall Mall. 1st Septr 1818.

Neckclothitania or Tietania
being an essay on Starchers
by one of the cloth.
J. J. Stockdale 1818.

𝕿rone d'Amour 𝕿ie.*

The *trone d'Amour* is the most austere after the Oriental Tie — It must be extremely well stiffened with starch.† It is formed by one single horizontal dent in the middle. Color, *Yeux de fille en extase.*

𝕴rish 𝕿ie.

This one resembles in some degree the Mathematical, with, however, this difference, that the horizontal indenture is placed *below* the point of junction formed by the collateral creases, instead of being above. The color, *Cerulean Blue.*

* So called from its resemblance to the Seat of Love.

† Starch is derived from the Teutonick word, "Starc" which means "stiff."

Ball Room Tie.

The Ball Room Tie when well put on, is quite delicious — It unites the qualities of the Mathematical and Irish, having two collateral dents and two horizontal ones, the one above as in the former, the other below as in the latter — It has no knot, but is fastened as the Napoleon. This should never of course be made with colors, but with the purest and most brilliant *blanc d'innocence virginale.*

Horse Collar Tie.

The Horse Collar has become, from some unaccountable reason, very universal. I can only attribute it to the inability of its wearers to make any other. It is certainly the worst and most vulgar, and I

102

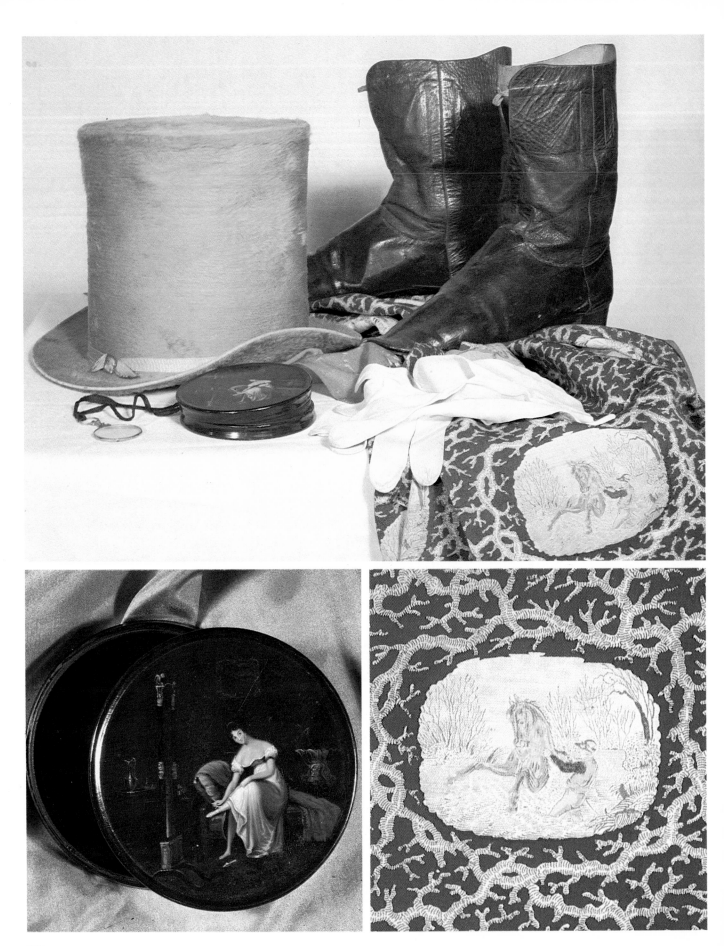

Fob chain with fobs. Various metals early 19th century.

Embroidered white cotton shirt with "J. White 1854" written in ink on lap. Tartan cut velvet waistcoat 1850-55. Shirt studs: painted paper portraits of ladies, behind glass mounted on gold coloured metal surrounds c.1850.

Opposite page
Above:
Silk plush hat, green and black boots with elastic pieces at top, cream knitted silk gloves, printed wool handkerchief, monocle and snuff box.
Early 19th century.
Left: Details of printed motif on handkerchief and snuff box.

Right: Blue and white cotton
waistcoat with woven pattern of
grasses 1840-1860.
Below left: Braces with kid and
elastic webbing ends and straps
embroidered in tent stitch by
Frances Leigh Killet
(1820-1908) for her fiancé
William Henry Bellot in 1847.
Below: Pale blue watered
silk stock c.1850.

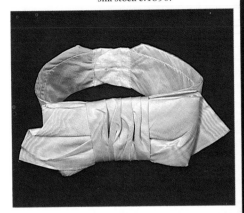

Photographs of gents
Top left: Daguerrotype c.1860.
Top right: Paper print by Walton
and Son, Margate c.1860-70.
Below left: Paper print 1860.
Below right: Paper print by
Webber and Bizzard, Taunton
1865-70.
Above: Foreign gent:
by H. Le Lieure,
Jardin Public, Turin.
Paper print c.1860.

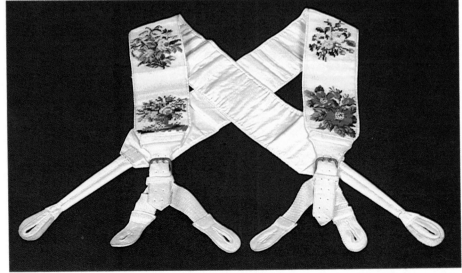

Shopping for Clothes 1770-1870

English Trades 1824 — The Linen Draper

"The Linen-Draper sells cloths which are made of flax and hemp; as Irish linens, Russia Towelling, Cambrics, etc., and, also, shawls, printed calicoes, muslin etc., etc. In London, it is, in the number of its articles, much more circumscribed than it is in the country, combining with their trade that of a silk-mercer, whereas, in London, these two trades are wholly distinct. The Linen-Draper is now comprehended under two, or at most, three distinct branches. We have the *Linen-Merchant,* a person whose more immediate province is to import articles of linen manufacture from foreign countries. We have also, the *Wholesale Linen-Draper;* a person whose business is to purchase linens from the merchant, and muslins, calicoes, printed cottons, etc., from the different manufacturers in Manchester, Blackburn, Paisley, etc. and to sell them to the retail linen drapers throughout the Kingdom, as well as frequently for exportation. The most striking part, however, is the *Retail Linen-Draper.*

We believe there is no trade in England, in which more efforts are made to captivate the public, and more especially the ladies, by a display of goods; and in London, this display is carried to a most costly and sumptuous extent. In most of the principle streets of the metropolis, shawls, muslins, pieces for ladies' dresses, and a variety of other goods, are shown with the assistance of mirrors, and at night by chandeliers, aided by the brilliancy which the gaslights afford, in a way almost as dazzling to a stranger, as many of those poetical fictions of which we read in the Arabian nights entertainment.

If, some years ago, our neighbours in sneer called us a nation of shopkeepers, we think that they must now give us the credit of being shopkeepers of taste, we apprehend no place in the world affords so great a variety of elegant amusement to the eye, as London in its various shops, and amongst these, those of the Linen-Draper are at all times conspicuous."

The Linen Draper from
*The Book of English Trades
and Library of Useful Arts*
Sir Richard Phillips and Co.
12th edition 1824.

For many people at the start of our period, shopping for clothes was a serious and expensive business. Since very few main outer garments were sold ready-made, this often meant in fact, buying the fabric, trimmings, linings and thread to be made up at home, or given to a dressmaker or tailor. Textiles were comparatively much more expensive than they are today, since so many of the processes were carried out by hand. For the average person, buying a material for a garment was a special event—it would be made to last many years, and then perhaps cut down for the children, or re-styled to squeeze a few more seasons' wear out of it. People in remote areas bought their material from travelling salesmen. The traveller remembered by Flora Thompson at the end of the century, was one of a rapidly dying breed.

Harding, Howell & Co.'s
Grand Fashionable Magazine, No. 89 Pall-Mall

Harding, Howell and Co's
Grand Fashionable Magazine,
No. 89 Pall-Mall *Ackermann's Repository of Arts* 1809.
Vol 1 No 3. p.187.

These premises, together with the two adjoining houses, formed, upwards of a century ago, the residence of the Duke of Schomberg, a Dutch general, who, at the revolution which placed the crown on the head of William the Third, accompanied that monarch to England, and fell by the fire of his own troops at the battle of the Boyne.

The house is one hundred and fifty feet in length from front to back, and of proportionate width. It is fitted up with great taste, and is divided by glazed partitions into four departments, for the various branches of the extensive business which is there carried on.

Immediately at the entrance is the first department, which is exclusively appropriated to the sale of furs and fans. The second contains articles of haberdashery of every description, silks, muslins, lace, gloves, etc. In the third shop, on the right, you meet with a rich assortment of jewellery, ornamental articles in ormolu, French clocks, etc., and on the left, with all the different kinds of perfumery necessary for the toilette. The fourth is set apart for millinery and dresses; so that there is no article of female attire or decoration, but what may be here procured in the first style of elegance and fashion.

This concern was founded twenty-five years since, by Messrs Dyde and Scribe, and has been conducted for the last twelve years by the present proprietors, who have spared neither trouble nor expense to ensure the establishment a superiority over every other in Europe, and to render it perfectly unique in its kind.

Forty persons are regularly employed on the premises in making up the various articles offered for sale, and in attendance on the different departments; while the number of artisans engaged in supplying the concern with novelties, almost exceeds belief.
Their exertions are rewarded by a successful introduction of all articles of merit among the first circles, by which they receive a certain stamp of fashion, and a consequent wide and general circulation through the country, to the great advantage of the manufacturer.

There is scarcely a manufacturing town in the kingdom but what it is laid under contribution by this establishment, the attention of whose spirited proprietors is not confined to native productions, but extends to every article of foreign manufacture which there is any possibility of obtaining.

Ackermann's Repository of Arts, Literature and Commerce, 1809 vol 1 No 3.

"The packman, or pedlar, once a familiar figure in that part of the country, was seldom seen in the 'eighties . . . but one last survivor of the once numerous clan, still visited the hamlet at long and irregular intervals.

He would turn aside from the turnpike and come plodding down the narrow hamlet road, an old white-headed, white bearded man, still hale and rosy, although almost bent double under the heavy, black canvas-covered pack he carried strapped on his shoulders. "Anything out of the pack today?" he would ask at each house, and at the least encouragement, fling down his load and open it on the doorstep. He carried a tempting variety of goods: dress-lengths and shirt-lengths and remnants to make up for children; aprons and pinafores, plain and fancy; corduroys for the men, and coloured scarves and ribbons for Sunday wear. "That's a bit of right good stuff, ma'am, that is" he would say, holding up some dress length to exhibit it. "A gown made of this piece'd last anybody for ever and then make 'em a good petticoat afterwards." Few of the hamlet women could afford to test the quality of his piece goods; cottons or tapes, or a paper of pins, were their usual purchases; but his dress-lengths and other fabrics were of excellent quality and wore much longer than anyone would wish anything to wear in these days of rapidly changing fashions. It was from his pack the soft, warm woollen, grey with a white fleck in it, came to make the frock Laura wore with a little black satin apron and a bunch of snowdrops pinned to the breast when she went to sell stamps in the Post Office."

Flora Thompson *Lark Rise to Candleford* 1945

These men were once a common enough sight on the turnpike roads—their packs full of Welsh flannel, Scottish or Irish linen, or the new and alluring printed cottons turned out by the huge mills of Manchester and Lancashire. On market days these pedlars, also known as Manchestermen, Scotchmen, or Talleymen, could be found in the large towns, selling their wares alongside stallholders. On a family trip to market, the housewife could visit the drapers' shops beginning to be seen and commented on by the late 18th century. Drapers differed from other shopkeepers in that they did not make their stock, but bought it from wholesalers in big cities. They needed a lot of capital and expertise to set up, and since their skill lay in selling rather than making, they sold vigorously. The trade was renowned for its advertising, its eyecatching window and door displays and its go ahead methods.

E. E. Perkins' *Treatise on Haberdashery and Hosiery* was in print from the 1830s to the 1870s. It was intended as a list of the complete range of goods available, as a guide to small drapers, their apprentices, and the general public. Successive editions gave wider and wider choices, not only of fabrics and haberdashery, but of the growing numbers of ready-made garments available, such as stockings, stays, hats, shoes and shirts. The 1845 edition is in the Platt Hall library, and makes fascinating reading: in many cases the range of goods was wider than it is today. For instance, twelve kinds of tapes are listed: Manchester "(or Incle, and sometimes called Beggars)", Holland, Scotch, Dutch, Imperial, Dutch Draper, Imperial Draper, Black, Blue, Pink, Axminster and Stay. Most were available in ten or more widths.

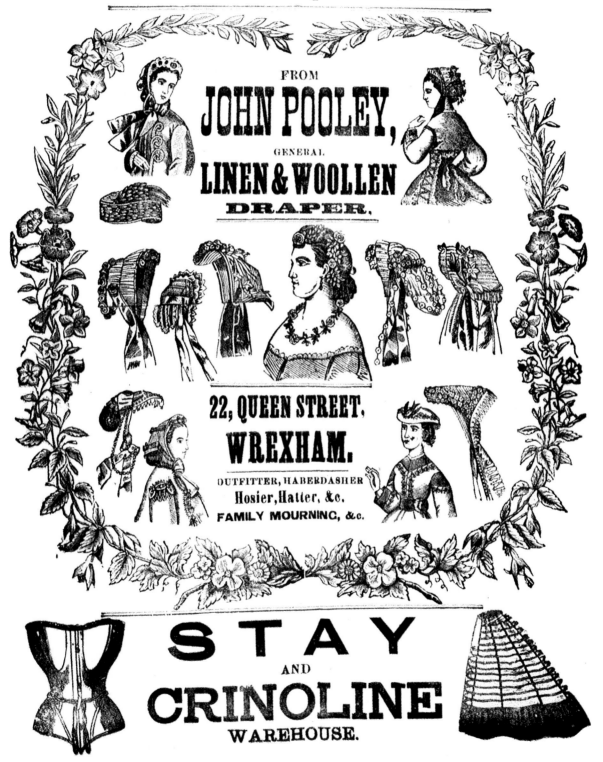

Is this the oldest paper-bag in the world? From the shop of John Pooley, Wrexham — Woodcut c.1865

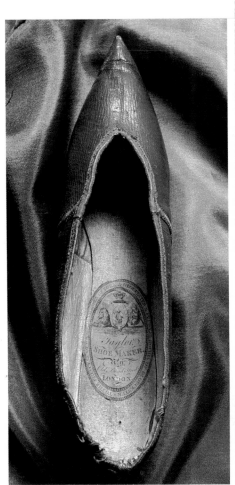

Red Morocco leather shoe with red silk binding—written inside in a contemporary hand "Her Grace Duchess of Hamilton" and paper label inside gives maker as Taylor, 9 Old Bond Street. Late 18th century.

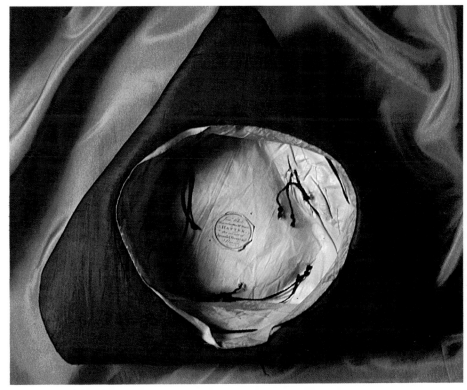

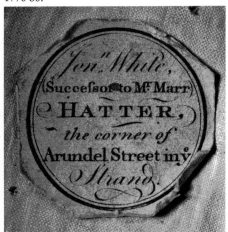

Man's hat—black silk over beaver felt, lined white linen. Belonged to Thomas Carill Worsley 1739-1809 who lived in Platt Hall 1759-1809. Made by Jonathan White, corner of Arundel Street and the Strand 1770-80.

The City of London was the home of the wholesale drapery trade, particularly the area around Wood Street and Saint Paul's Churchyard.

Small shopkeepers flocked there from all over the country, especially after the introduction of railways, and were there subjected to sales talk as effective as their own. Many of the warehouses were run by country manufacturers; hosiers like I. & R. Morley of Nottingham, or glovers like Dent Allcroft and Co. of Worcester, had warehouses very early in the century, where they sold not only their own products, but rapidly diversified into such lines as shirts, neckwear, handkerchiefs or parasols.

At this time, different types of ready-made clothing were made in specialised localities. Felt hats were produced in Manchester and its outskirts; especially Stockport and Denton. In Manchester itself, cotton goods like shirts were manufactured. Manchester was also the home of the Macintosh: Charles Macintosh had been financed by the Birley brothers, cotton manufacturers, and had set up his factory there in 1823, to make waterproof fabric by sandwiching a sheet of rubber between two pieces of cloth, and then later making garments from it. Leather gloves came from Worcester and the West Country. Shoes were made at Street, in Somerset, by Cyrus and James Clark, as well as in Northampton. All kinds of hosiery came from Nottingham, Leicester and Derby, but Nottingham specialised in fine silk goods, and machine made lace, which was originally derived from hosiery technology, whereas Leicester was known for its woollens, such as jackets, shawls and mittens.

The manufacturer's name is known to us even less often than that of the wearer of a garment, but printed paper labels can be found stuck in small objects, dating as far back as the late 18th century.

Both the hat and shoe shown here would have been custom-made, rather than mass-produced. This means of self advertisement was equally useful in both areas. Hosiers often knitted their mark into goods, and printed their name on stocking feet. The practice of putting woven labels into garments began in the mid 19th century, but early examples are very rare.

"Getting into Very Low Habits" — The clothiers Moses and Son ridiculed in *Punch* 1843, Vol. V, p.249.

The areas around ports traditionally specialised in "slop-work"; cheap, basic clothing for sailors, for export to the colonies, and to provide emigrants with complete outfits to last a lifetime. This trade expanded to include all kinds of ready-made clothing for the general public. Portsmouth and Bristol were producers of women's underwear, especially corsets and crinolines, whereas at Liverpool, and the East End of London, tailored garments were made.

By the 1840s the East End was thronged with tailors, relying on poor immigrants working in sweat shops to turn out trousers, coats and jackets at ridiculously low prices. One of the best known of these houses was that of Elias Moses and Son of the Minories and Aldgate. Throughout the 1840s and 1850s they published self advertising pamphlets with names like *The Record of Public Sentiments* (1855) *The Commercial Cornucopia* (1855) or *The Pillars of Trade* (1856), in which they list their prices and show their range of goods. (*Punch* ridiculed these, reviewing them as if they were serious literature, and Mayhew was to reveal the true horror of their employees' working conditions.)

Experiments were being made with measuring systems, and some degree of fit was increasingly possible. However, most respectable people continued to despise ready made clothes, since they so often looked as if they belonged to someone else. Clothiers were also looked down upon for their "revolutionary" practices; such as ticketing every garment with a fixed price "to which no abatement can be made", allowing casual browsers to visit their spacious showrooms without obligation, and offering a money-back guarantee.

Such firms were hugely successful, attracting a clientele from all sections of society, and maintaining branches both in Britain and abroad.

If E. Moses and Son were the 19th century equivalent of today's menswear chains, then other shops were prototypes for the modern department store. Jay's Mourning Warehouse on Regent Street was opened in 1841, and sold everything that was considered necessary for a stylish funeral and bereavement. Since this covered many aspects of dress, as well as areas such as stationery, the shop had numerous departments and workrooms.

Jays Mourning Warehouse box with 1868 written in contemporary hand. Jays bill 2.3.1867 to Mrs. C. Worsley, Thompson Hotel, Holles Street "Bonnet £1.15.6. and fronts 4s. . . ." Mourning handkerchiefs mid 19th century.

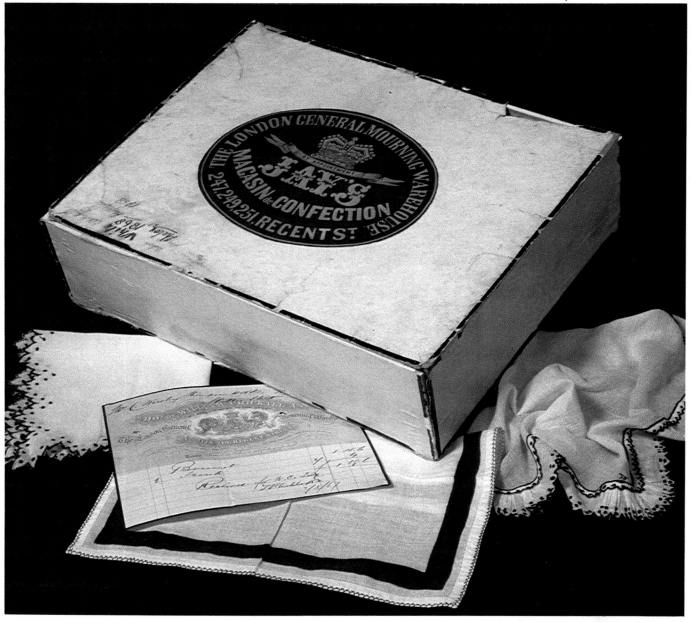

115

One of the earliest shops which undoubtedly deserved the title of "department store" was Manchester's Kendal Milne and Faulkner. Set up by John Watts, a farmer and weaver, in 1796, to sell his own fabric, by the 1820s "The Bazaar" as it was known, housed a collection of stalls on two storeys hired out to different people. In *Shops and Shopping*, Alison Adburgham reproduces the 1831 prospectus of "The Bazaar" which stated:

"The great object in the general arrangement of this bazaar is to promote the reciprocal interests of Purchaser and Vendors, to give employment to industrious Females, and at the same time to secure to the Public the choicest and most fashionable Articles in every branch of Art and Manufacture at a reasonable rate."

The tenants had to agree to abide by the house rules: the bazaar was to be open from 9.30 am to 8 pm. The tenants were to deal only in those goods agreed by the manager; the prices should be marked on the goods; the tenants should be clean and well dressed; females were not allowed "to have their hair in papers, or to wear bonnets"; neither gossiping nor eating was allowed behind the counters.

In the early 1830s, Thomas Kendal, James Milne and Adam Faulkner joined the management of the bazaar, and the three bought out the Watts family in 1836. The firm traded not only in items essential for the lady of fashion, but upholstery and carpets, cabinet making, funeral undertaking and mourning goods. Kendals still exists and prospers today. Since the first world war it was owned by Harrods of Knightsbridge, and was purchased with the Harrods group by House of Fraser in 1959. A collection of bills belonging to the Worsley family has survived at Platt Hall, dating from the 1850s to the 1870s, and these include a wide variety of items bought at Kendals.

Opposite page:
Bills for haberdashery bought from Kendal Milne and Faulkner Manchester 1857 to 1858.

Below:
Man's Stock c.1840. Black satin with red silk lining bearing label printed on cream silk. G. Baker and Company, Hosiers, Glovers and Shirtmaker, Manufacturers of Military and Dress Stocks, Cravats etc. 3 and 4 Ludgate Hill. London.

Houlstons Industrial Library
The Draper and Haberdasher J. W. Hayes 1878

p.11
The Requirements etc., of the drapery trade.
Let us now proceed to consider what is required of those who enter this
calling, and the qualifications of body and mind that it demands . . .
Courtesy—In the first place, any youth who would do well in this vocation,
should ask himself if he is fairly free from those infirmities of temper which
so often mar man's passage through life, or if he be not, if he possesses
sufficient self-restraint and mastery over himself to struggle against them.
The hours are long and wearisome, especially to the young; the work is tiring
too, and though it may not involve any strained mental attention, as many
callings do, it brings with it every moment, a considerable amount of petty
labour in searching for various articles that are asked for, bringing forward to
be looked at, tying, unfolding, displaying, folding up, tying up once again, and
finally restoring the goods to the place whence they were taken.
And sometimes it may happen that all this may be done fruitlessly over and
over again, without effecting so much as the sale of a yard of ribbon . . .

p.13
Cleanliness . . . the very work of handling so many parcels, whose envelopes
and wrappings will unavoidably afford a lodgment for dust, and so many
materials, will soon soil the hands, but soap and water are never far off, and an
interval in the business of the day will frequently occur, when the hands can
be washed. A lady will infinitely prefer to have goods placed before her by
a pair of hands that are clean and well kept, than with hands that are dingy in
hue, disfigured with ragged nails tipped with blackened rims, and clasped at
the wrists by cuffs or wristbands of doubtful colour.

p.15
. . . Of a truth, Courtesy, Cleanliness, Punctuality and Honesty, may be called
the Cardinal Virtues of a business life, for if a man have these, he will not fail,
we think, to have the others also, which are so near akin to these.

p.23
Haberdashery. Smallwares are often left to the care of an apprentice or Junior,
and kept in some out of the way place, and seldom thought of, except when
asked for. Then customers are often served with careless reluctance, as if a
favour were conferred on them.

p.25
. . . Go into what town you will, large or small, there are to be found numbers
of little haberdashery and hosiery shops . . . the owners have never been
brought up in the trade, but are self-educated. In many instances they first
commenced by buying a few shillings worth, which they dearly purchased from
the draper. This small stock they have shown in their shop windows, and sold
at extra profit to the actual customers who are neglected by the very draper
the goods in the first place came from. By degrees they increase their stock,
are called upon by smallware travellers, learn the business better than the
draper himself, become independent of him, and succeed in establishing a
thriving business, not only in smallwares, but in hosiery, gloves, lace, and
other fancy goods, all to the loss of the draper, who often wonders why his
returns in hosiery and gloves are so small in proportion to his general trade.
In Manchester, Liverpool and London and other large towns, within a stone's
throw of drapers, are large haberdashery shops turning over thousands yearly.

p.28
Every apprentice should be well educated in haberdashery before he is allowed
to serve in the general drapery.

p.29

The haberdashery drawers should be frequently dusted out, kept well assorted, and the contents arranged in successive numbers from left to right or right to left, but avoid changing . . . When colours are arranged in braids, reel cotton, or sewing silks, never put purple by the side of blue, or blue by green, let some other colour intervene, the shades can then be more readily distinguished by gas light.

p.30

Wholesale warehousemen in London and Manchester have goods got up with their names on the brand, representing them to be made expressly by or for them. Any draper can, if he likes, to some extent, do the same, but it is not a desirable plan. Small shop keepers or hawkers, who might buy from you, do not like to tell their customers where to buy their goods . . . There are some few manufacturers of sewing cotton, knitting cotton, needles and pins, whose goods are well known to the public, and the warehouseman is bound to keep them.

p.33

Tying parcels. It is good plan to have a few hooks in some convenient place, so that each piece of twine can be hung up by the loop in different lengths, ready for use when required.

p.34

. . . when a small packet is opened, and only part of the contents are wanted, see that it is opened at the right end, without destroying the front label, it can then be repacked and placed in position, without the appearance of having been opened.

Customers' parcels — Goods when sold should be neatly and firmly packed. Very small packets may be finished with a twist of paper at one end, but if over six inches in length they should be secured round the centre, larger parcels in the usual way.

p.36

Farthings — It is a common practice in most parts of England, to give a small ball of sewing cotton or a few pins, by way of change in lieu of odd farthings. This plan is objectionable, as is also that of giving what is called "good measure", because it is often a source of loss to employers . . . the farthing cotton balls, and the "good measure" are of little or no value to those who receive them, whereas farthings soon make pennies, and pennies shillings, and so on.

p.37

Ventilation Avoid keeping coloured goods in high fixtures, where the gas is apt to damage them; low fixtures are preferable, especially now that so many ladies are employed in the business. Shop and window ventilation are very much neglected; considerable loss consequently arises from goods coming in contact with condensed vapour.

p.41

Window dressing, including arrangements of colours, is an important part of an assistant's duties. No hand can become expert in this art without practice; moreover, he must be really interested in what he is doing, or he cannot excel. The object of window-dressing is, of course, to attract purchasers.
A man who expects, from the position of his shop, to do a low class trade, will not dress his window as if it were situated in an aristocratic thoroughfare.
To obtain an effective display, the glass should be perfectly clean, and the colours arranged with due regard to the laws of harmony and contrast . . .
Much also depends on the manner goods are arranged. Any boy can place them in a window, but it requires familiar knowledge, united to readiness of performance, to place them in effective position, which can only be arrived at by frequent practice.

Jay's Mourning Warehouse
Billhead. c.1850.

AL MOURNING
SE.

FOR COURT, FAMILY,
OR
COMPLIMENTARY MOURNING.

& C°.

NT STREET.

S MAKING.

Working Class Clothing

Woman "buddling" (ore-dressing) at a Cornish tin-mine. Her bonnet is in the fashion of the 1840's but her bedgown and petticoat are the costume worn by countrywomen since the 18th century.
Useful Arts and Manufactures Second selection 1850 (published by The Society for Promotion of Christian Knowledge.)

Museums are often asked about working class dress, and about regional costume, and we find these questions particularly complex and difficult to answer.

What did factory children wear at the time of the Industrial Revolution? The answers "whatever their mothers could afford", or "a ragged version of what other children wore" may be near the truth, but seem unsatisfactory. Our mental picture of the past would be tidier if we could imagine a society where dress was exactly matched to status, region and occupation.

But nineteenth century Britain presented a far less orderly appearance. New industries demanded new workforces, while advances in technology made other skills redundant. The population was now congregated in the cities, and communications and transport were the best in the world. There were few isolated communities where a regional style could fossilise and be called traditional. Nevertheless, even in a state of profound social change, groups of workers in a particular industry and a particular locality may have adopted a special way of dressing, and it is the job of museums and libraries to find and preserve the evidence.

Museum costume collections have a bias towards the wealthy middle classes, and to fashionable and designer clothing. So little remains of the dress of the poor that there is no possibility of preserving and presenting a complete cross-section of society. Certain working garments have an aesthetic appeal that has ensured their survival—countrymen's smocks and rural sunbonnets are a good example. One or two occupations have a special hold on the imagination, and their way of life and dress have been well documented—the knitting patterns of fisherfolk have been widely studied and revived; the canal boatwomen were much photographed and their costume perhaps became "traditional" because of its picturesque and independent appearance. But there are many trades which never had the distinction of special dress, many occupations so unglamorous that only the committed social observer photographed or commented on them. For them we have to rely on a variety of sources: engravings, newspaper and magazine articles, official reports, memoirs and diaries, photographs and occasionally paintings. The personal recollections of elderly people are a priceless record of the past.

The Gallery of English Costume collects both urban and rural dress, and tries to keep a social balance. Everyday things, even modern ones, are treated with as much respect as high fashion. Small drapers' shops which are closing down are a good source of mass-produced twentieth century goods: overalls, agricultural corduroys, little boys' cheap suits, even wartime Utility corsets, can be found with their price labels intact. Yet though they give a picture of what was available, and at what price, these unworn clothes lack the impact of garments that have been mended, washed, lived in.

Previous Page.
Top Left:
Yellow Hannah "Poor old woman—lived in a lodging house. Called 'Yellow Hannah' because of her complexion. Came to the Vicarage often for soup and used tea leaves". Handwritten note on the back of the carte de visite taken by T. B. Mellor, Belper, 1860s.

Top right:
Mary Dent, Skelton Mary Dent is probably a cook or cook-maid. Cooks wore apron, cap, and sometimes over-sleeves, for hygiene's sake, although by the 1860s caps were going out of fashion for the young. She has pinned up her skirt, revealing a striped petticoat, to save her silk dress from splashes. The silk dress may have been put on for the photograph.

Bottom left:
Miners from Tredegar The one on the right has a candle in his hat, a frequent method of illumination, long after the invention of the Davy safety lamp (1815). A naked flame invited accidents in fire-damp pits.
Photo: W. Clayton, Iron St. Tredegar. 1860s.

Bottom right:
Unknown Fisherman This studio portrait probably shows him in his best clothes, not his working gear. His guernsey (gansey) is knitted in the pattern known as "Betty Martin"; she is said to have been a Filey knitter, but the pattern appears to have been used in many regions.
Photo: J. Usher, Ramsgate, 1860s.

Right:
Wigan pit-brow girls in trousers, with petticoats pinned up.
Photograph by J. Cooper, Standishgate, Wigan. 1860s.

From the eighteenth and nineteenth century, clothes with a documented working class background rarely survive. Platt Hall has a good collection of rural clothing, like smocks, and the bedgown and red cloak of the village woman. But in the next pages we are going to look at the clothes of female workers in industrial centres like Manchester and South Wales, and at the second hand clothes trade which was both the origin and eventual fate of much everyday clothing.

The Heavy Industries: Coal and Iron.

The Coalmines Regulation Act, 1842, put an end to the underground labour of women and children, and they no longer spent their working lives drawing wagons along the tunnels like human pit-ponies. Nevertheless, women continued as surface workers, and their labour was arduous enough.
In iron and coal districts they were employed on the tips and pit-banks to load and unload waggons. The usual shift was twelve hours, 6.00 to 6.00.
Tools were a pick or lump hammer to break up the blocks of coal and iron-ore, a shovel to load the wagons, a riddle to sort the lumps, an oil can to grease the wheels.

The employment of women in heavy industry became a subject for heated debate in the second half of the nineteenth century. The practice was considered degrading to the female sex on medical and social grounds; furthermore it was condemned from that universal Victorian viewpoint, fear of indecency and immorality. It could be argued that dirty manual toil for twelve hours a day would leave one ill-prepared for a life of sin, yet this was one of the most frequently aired objections. It did, at least, ensure the matter a good hearing and a lot of publicity. Girls were said to use foul language, to flirt and backchat with their male workmates, to make shiftless wives and, too often, unmarried mothers. It should be said that there is little evidence that they were any more prone to these evils than other working women.

Platt Hall has material from two areas of Britain where female labour was commonplace, the coal tips of Wigan and the iron works of South Wales. The dress of these women shows interesting regional variations, and the documents from Wales give an insight into the minds of the objectors to, and defenders of, the practice of employing women labourers.

The Wigan Pit Brow Girls.

The Wigan girls became a cause célèbre in the debate on female labour, partly because of their distinctive style of dress. They worked in trousers.
This was deeply shocking to Victorian sensibilities. In the 1860's at the height of this controversy, the fashionable dress was the crinoline.
For walking, and games like croquet, it was permissible for young ladies to display a little ankle in bright stockings. But the attempts of the American Mrs. Bloomer to introduce "bifurcated garments" were a nine days' wonder of the 1850's, and the rational dress movement did not gain ground until the end of the century.

Outsiders considered the trousers of the Wigan pit brow girls to be utterly degrading. Trousers on the one hand were thought to be unfeminine, making the girls coarse and mannish in their behaviour, and on the other hand to be provocative, doubtless leading to immorality and ruin.

The Wigan girls had a champion and admirer in Arthur Munby, a gentleman who found himself irresistibly attracted to independent minded and handsome working women, and indeed to the whole notion of female labour. His diaries and photographs in the library of Trinity College, Cambridge, give a vivid and personal account of his visits to Wigan and conversations with the pit brow girls. Munby's papers have been the inspiration for two recent books (Michael Hiley *Victorian Working Women: Portraits from Life* and Derek Hudson *Munby: Man of Two Worlds*), and it would be foolish to attempt to add to their research in these few pages. However, Munby's enthusiasm for his subject throws light on material in the Platt Hall collection.

The notoriety and publicity attached to the Wigan girls' dress made them a popular subject for local photographers. It appears that cartes de visite (small album photos) were sold as souvenirs and curiosities; they were presumably also kept as records by social reformers, and used as sources for engraved magazine illustrations. One such photograph has found its way into Dr. Cunnington's collection.

A more unusual and exciting record of the Wigan girls' dress was brought into Platt Hall by a member of the public in 1981. This is a doll, kept as a family treasure, but unfortunately having no history or legend to go with her. The doll was cleaned and conserved in Platt Hall, and was displayed in the gallery, but has now returned to her owners, who have given us permission to publish her picture.

The Wigan doll must have been made in the 1860's, and is clearly intended as an accurate record of the pit women's dress. Her clothes are made of authentic materials, and bear out Munby's description fairly closely: "A hooded bonnet of padded cotton, pink blue or black; a blue striped shirt open at the breast; a waistcoat of cloth, generally double-breasted, but ragged and patched throughout; fustian or corduroy or sometimes blackcloth trousers, patched with all possible materials except the original ones; and stout clog shoon, brassclasped, on their bare feet; round the waist is tucked a petticoat of striped cotton, blue and black, rolled up as a joiner rolls up his apron; it is never let down, and it is perfectly useless—only retained as a symbol of sex." (Munby's Diary for Friday 19 August 1859).

The doll's bonnet and blouse are yellow and white striped. Her petticoat is not cotton, but drugget, a material with cotton warp and woollen weft, with weft stripes of grey, blue and scarlet. This fabric was used for the skirts of many working women; mill-hands and bondagers (farm-workers of the Scottish borders) wore drugget skirts, and some survive in museum collections as unsold shop-stock, probably from the time of the Great War. Indeed a fashion magazine unknowingly promoted working womens' petticoats in the autumn of 1982; a London antique market was selling them as peasant skirts.

The doll's waistcoat had detachable cloth sleeves, one now being lost and the other badly damaged. They were presumably for bad weather, but none of Munby's photographs shows them in use. It is likely that the cloth waistcoat was made from a second-hand male garment such as a coat. Her trousers are of cream flannel with a fluffy nap, and Munby mentions flannel trousers elsewhere in his account. The doll's shovel has the maker's name cast in the blade, "Clarington Brook Forge", a place still known to Wigan residents.

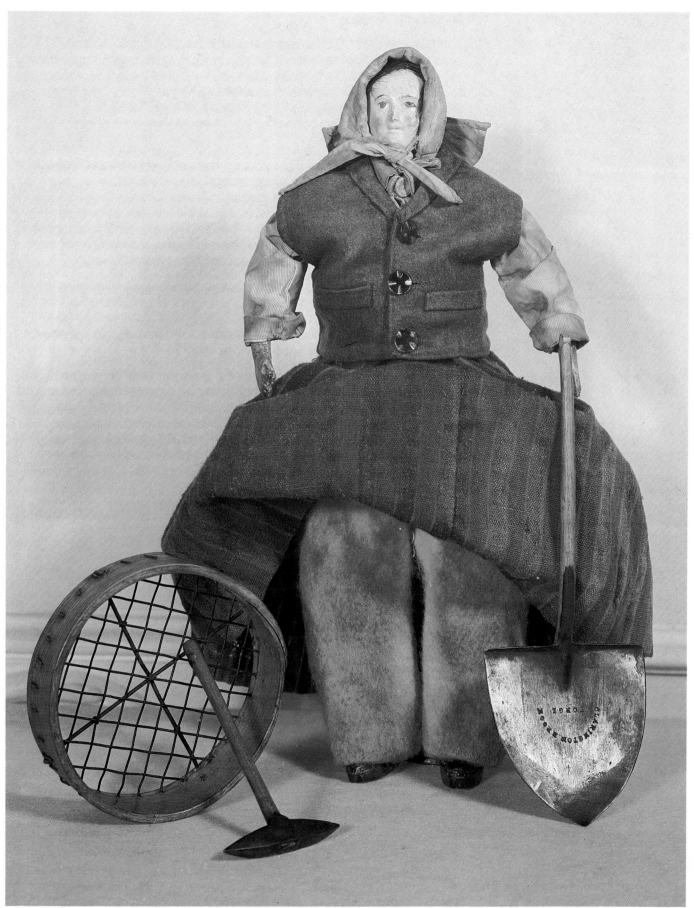

Doll, dressed in the 1860s to represent a Wigan pit-brow worker. Private collection; conserved at Platt Hall.

Welsh Iron Workers

The trousers of the Wigan pit girls were practical, warm and comfortable, giving freedom of movement and being less likely to get trapped in machinery and cause accidents. Nevertheless there are no accounts of women habitually wearing trousers in other branches of industry elsewhere in Britain, although some fisherwomen pinned up their petticoats 'bloomer' fashion.
In Belgium, however, where women still worked underground, they wore trousers down the pit.

At the iron works of South Wales, in the region of Blaenavon and Tredegar, women loaded coke and broke up ironstone, work similar to that of their Wigan counterparts. Yet their lot appears to have excited less publicity and controversy, and it is difficult to escape the conclusion that this is partly due to their more conventional attire. Munby paid only fleeting visits to the area and did not form the strong attachment he felt for Wigan. Platt Hall is therefore extremely fortunate in having rare documents from South Wales.

Among the Cunnington collection is an album of cartes de visite taken by W. Clayton, a professional photographer from Iron Street, Tredegar.
The album is prefaced by a newspaper cutting from the *Bristol Mercury*, 29 April, 1865, part of which is reproduced here with some of the photographs. The album is signed "C. B. Crisp 29 April 1865".

The Welsh women look more ragged and camera-shy than the Wigan girls. It is unwise to generalise from photographs, but we can infer that the women of Tredegar were less used to publicity. From Munby's account the Wigan girls appear as a close-knit and cheerful group, but we can be less sure of the characters of these shadowy figures. Munby ensured that the names and personalities of some of his favorites were handed down to posterity, like Ellen Grounds and Jane Brown (Jaan Brahn). The Welsh workers have no such identification.

When the library of Platt Hall was recently reorganised a new document relating to the iron workers came to light. This is a small notebook, compiled by the same C. B. Crisp, containing newspaper cuttings of a heated correspondence in the columns of the *Merthyr Telegraph* (Jan-Feb 1865) on the question "Should Female Labour be Employed in the Iron Works?"
We do not know who C. B. Crisp was, but we believe that he/she was a reformer interested in founding a Female Protection Society to improve the conditions of these women.

The correspondence is too long for this book, but a few extracts will give the flavour of some of the arguments. All the letter-writers used pen-names, and it is probable that they were all men. Nowhere is the opinion of the workers themselves quoted.

"W" points out that where women work in industry, fewer are available for domestic service:
"The girls employed in the Iron Works have their liberty after the work is done. They have three or four hours every night after six o'clock to do as they please, and if working at night have a few hours in the early morning for a stroll and a gossip. But the female domestic servant . . . must not leave the house; or if she be sent on an errand she is expected to return immediately. No "followers" are allowed, and perhaps no holiday for the first six months . . . Working men complain that their wives are of very little use to them as help-meets. They can't make their children's clothes and they can't cook . . . As long as women are taught to handle the crowbar we cannot expect them to be expert with their needles."

Opposite and overleaf:
Photographs of Welsh Ironworkers, by W. Clayton, Iron St. Tredegar c.1865.

"Mercator" is obviously an employer:

"If females are employed, it is no fault of the masters . . . They use no compulsion to force females to labour in their works . . . no law is broken, and no principles set at defiance."

"Philanthropy" advocates the formation of a Female Protection Society, and his comments illustrate the radical distinction between a 'female' and a 'lady':

"I invite the ladies to ply their needles and their talents in preparing pretty little articles and ornaments; start bazaars, and ask the ladies to preside—gentlemen will always support the fair sex in these matters . . ."

"Medicus" writes as a professional man:

"The employment of the physically weak in labours demanding great physical exertion, tends to lessen the capacity of throwing off diseases, and gradually dwarfs the physical frame . . . when these females become the mothers of the succeeding generation, we find the offspring debilitated by the weakness of the parent. This may account in some degree for the large number of infantile deaths beyond the average of other places."

"Q" appears to be a radical and a moralist, and makes some practical suggestions:

"Our first object should be to gain the goodwill of the employers themselves . . . They must see that hard work is degrading in its effects upon the female character . . . that illegitimacy is increased by the contact of female with male labour, that the infant death rate must always be high . . . No infirmaries founded by Ironmasters grace the town, no churches or chapels built at their expense . . . If a balance were struck between the stoppages of the workmen, and the expenditure on their account for medicine and education, there would be a pretty considerable surplus in favour of the workmen . . . First, get the masters to keep a strict watch over these poor girls while they are engaged at work . . . to deal as severely as they can with every instance where a gaffer has abused his position to effect his own base designs . . . To erect public conveniences in the works for the females . . . Next the proposed Society should agitate Parliament for an extension of the Factory Acts to this district."

Female Labour in the Welsh Iron Works

"Travellers see strange sights, and strangers coming into the Iron districts of South Wales often make strange remarks. It is, however, a fine sight at night to see the blaze issuing from the numberless fires of the Tredegar Iron Works, illuminating the sky far over the distant hills. These immense works occupy a large area of ground and employ several thousand hands and continually send forth flames from furnaces burning some hundred tons of coal.

Surrounding the town and the works are what strangers call the "Black Mountains" which are the refuse and burnt coal tipped and heaped together from the works, and, being accumulated, forms in the course of time a range of semi-mountains, until these tips consolidate and get covered with verdure, and on part of some of the old tips, George-town, Vale Terrace, and rows of houses have lately been built. On the top of these tips, rails are laid down for trams, to carry away the useless mass of cinder from the fires and furnaces, and on arriving at the extremity, the trams are tipped and by this means the black mountains or tips are everlastingly on the increase in length and height. To do this work women and girls are employed and wear a peculiar style of dress, consisting of a short frock and apron, tight to the neck, made of a material resembling hop cloth or fine sacking, red worsted stockings and lace-up boots heavy with hobnails, tips and toecaps that would pull the legs off some of the ploughmen of the Midland Counties. The bonnet or hat, for it is difficult to discern to which of the classes this head-dress belongs, is bedecked with beads, brooches, and feathers, the latter addition in a small way imitating the Prince of Wales plume. In this dress, with faces black with dust and smoke, it is difficult, when elevated fifty or a hundred yards, to discern the sex to which these objects belong; and a gentleman, who evidently had never witnessed such a sight before, on visiting the town of Tredegar recently, expressed his astonishment at making mountains on mountains and inquired what animals those were he saw moving about on the top?

In the tempest and the storm, in rain and in snow, in the sun and heat, exposed to all weathers, women and young girls are employed on the tips in South Wales."

from the Bristol Mercury, *29 April 1865.*

The correspondence was closed in March 1865, with an editorial supporting the idea of a Female Protection Society, but expressing little faith in the power or the will of the legislature to do anything about it.

The topic of women in heavy industry continued to be debated, but the issue was a complex one. Against the arduousness and danger of their labour was set their right to work, and their avowed preference for an independent way of life. If the question can be said to have been resolved, it was by an increasing concern for health and safety, and by a succession of Acts regulating the working conditions of both men and women.

"Lucy, maid of all work, ? on her wedding day."

The alternative to employment in industry was usually domestic service, and it was often said that the manual workers preferred their independence to the life of a general servant.

Cassell's Household Guide gives an account of the duties of a maid of all work. "They know something of cooking . . . they understand housemaid's work, and have almost always begun by being nursemaids. Their wages vary . . . from seven or eight, to sixteen pounds a year. Sometimes the wages are modified by arrangements which require them to find their own tea and sugar, beer &c. . ."

"Lucy, maid of all work, *?* on her wedding day". Photograph, W. Darnell, Hammersmith. 1886.

Her plan of work began with early rising (6.00 at the latest); polishing, lighting the kitchen range and brushing out the flues; putting on the kettle and polishing knives and boots as the fire draws; cleaning and sweeping the breakfast parlour; cleaning and lighting the fire; sweeping the hall and whitening the doorstep; collecting and sifting the cinders; changing into clean clothes; dusting the breakfast room and laying the table; serving the family breakfast.

"If there be sufficient time, this is the best opportunity for her own breakfast. If not, she should manage to have her meal as soon as possible afterwards. Nothing tends to good humour so much as a sound digestion, and servants cannot be healthy if they snatch their food while running about."

The morning continued with cleaning the bedrooms and emptying chamber-pots, followed by a general washing up in the kitchen. "The mistress or daughters will probably in the meanwhile dust the ornaments in the drawing-room, and aid in giving an air of order and refinement to the room". Answering the door to tradesmen was an interruption, and it was advisable to arrange that they should call on specified days.

The main meal of the day was cooked and served by the maid, who then did the light washing up, saving the heavy things for the morning. "Under these circumstances the servant can wait upon the family in the evening, and employ the rest of her time in repairing or making her clothes." On Saturday she would soak the white linens in preparation for the Monday wash.

A maid of all work would be employed in a lower middle class household like Mr. Pooter's in *The Diary of a Nobody.* He once had to speak to his Sarah "about walking all over the drawing-room carpet with a piece of yellow soap on the heel of your boot."

Above:
Laundrymaid operating a mangle. She wears a small crinoline, and has pinned up her skirt to keep her dress dry. *Cassell's Household Guide.* (c.1870).

Right:
Cause and Effect Punch, March 26, 1864, poking fun at a servant's home-made attempts to be in fashion.

CAUSE AND EFFECT.

Housemaid. "DRAT THE BOTHERING CHINA CUPS AND THINGS. THEY BE ALWAYS A-KNOCKING UP AGAINST ONE'S CRINOLINE."

Lancashire Mill Workers

Eyre Crowe was criticised for portraying an urban working class subject in *The Dinner Hour, Wigan,* for this was generally considered unworthy of attention in art, if not in literature. The painting, now in Manchester City Art Gallery, is a rare and valuable record of working life, as well as a lively and attractive image. It is interesting that Crowe, like Munby, was drawn to Wigan for his material. Perhaps he, too, was attracted by the strong sense of local identity.

The girls in the painting are all rosy-cheeked and buxom, with not a hair out of place or a speck of cotton dust on them. Nevertheless, idealised though it is, this is still a well-observed picture giving vivid detail of working dress. No single pictorial source should be taken as unbiased evidence: engravings illustrating textbooks on trade and industry depict suspiciously orderly and safe-looking work-places, while it is a natural tendency of reforming works to concentrate on the black side. Even photographs can be composed to make a point.

DRESS.

OCTOBER 9th, 1860.

IT is always a pleasure to us to see our workpeople, and especially our comely young women, dressed NEAT and TIDY ; nor should we, as has been already declared in a notice that has been put up at Bocking Mills, wish to interfere with the fashion of their dress, whatever it may be, so long as their dress does not interfere with their work, or with the work of those near them in our employ.

The present ugly fashion of HOOPS, or CRINOLINE, as it is called, is, however, quite unfitted for the work of our Factories. Among the Power Looms it is almost impossible, and highly dangerous ; among the Winding and Drawing Engines it greatly impedes the free passage of Overseers, Wasters, &c., and is inconvenient to all. At the Mills it is equally inconvenient, and still more mischievous, by bringing the dress against the Spindles, while also it sometimes becomes shockingly indecent when the young people are standing upon the Sliders.

FOR ALL THESE REASONS

We now request all our Hands, at all our Factories, to leave HOOPS AND CRINOLINE at home when they come to the Factories to work ; and to come dressed in a manner suitable for their work, and with as much BECOMING NEATNESS as they can.

And OVERSEERS at all the Floors are hereby charged to see that all the Hands coming to work are thus properly dressed for factory work—without Hoops or Crinoline of any sort ; and Overseers will be held RESPONSIBLE to us for strict regard to this regulation.

Licking Bobbins.

WHEN a Bobbin is fastened off, it has been a common practice to touch the end with the tongue to smooth it down, and there is no harm in that.

But out of this practice has arisen another practice, both nasty and mischievous, of licking the Bobbins all over to make them weigh heavier.

And to put an end at once, and altogether, to this nasty and mischievous practice of Licking the Bobbins, we now make it

A RULE

Not to touch the Bobbins with the Tongue at all ; and Overseers are hereby authorised to enforce this rule by Forfeits.

SAMUEL COURTAULD & Co.

Notice, posted in Courtauld's Mills in 1860, prohibiting the wearing of crinolines on the factory floor, for safety reasons.

The factory girls wear short skirts, showing their calves in red or white stockings, and their buckled clogs with brass toe-caps. Their petticoats are brightly coloured (red, blue) or in drab tones, and some are striped like the skirt of the Wigan miner doll. The picture cannot give the texture of the petticoats, which might be of cotton or drugget. There are records of mill-workers wearing cotton print dresses, rather than petticoat and blouse, and when Miss Stanley visited a school for unemployed factory girls at Stockport in November 1862, she saw that "most of them had the usual factory girl's dress on, print gown and a shepherd's plaid put over their heads and pinned under their chins." The mill-girls at the Manchester Old Clothes Fair, in the picture on page 139, are wearing and trying on printed cotton dresses. Some of the Wigan factory girls are wearing short sleeved white cotton overalls, and the back view of one of them shows that she is wearing stays over a white chemise under her overall and skirt. The stays are laced so

"They were most of them factory girls, and wore the usual out-of-doors dress of that particular class of maidens; namely a shawl, which at mid-day or in fine weather was allowed to be merely a shawl, but towards evening, or if the day were chilly, became a sort of Spanish mantilla or Scotch plaid, and was brought over the head and hung loosely down, or was pinned under the chin in no unpicturesque fashion."

(Manchester girls, on a May evening holiday, from *Mary Barton: A Tale of Manchester Life* Mrs. Elizabeth Gaskell 1848)

that they can be tightened by the wearer herself, and exactly the same costume can be seen in the picture of the Old Clothes Market.

The workers wear their hair gathered up into chignons, and held in place by hair-nets. This may be a safety precaution, but we should remember that this was a very fashionable hairstyle in the 1860's. Some of the girls wear jewellery, coral beads and small gold earrings. Only two of them are barefoot.

Shawls, often with a woven check, like the shepherd's plaid Miss Stanley noticed, were worn either drawn up over the head, or round the neck, and were pinned at the throat. The shawl was usually folded in a rectangle, not in the triangular manner of a fashionable shawl. Surviving examples often show the marks of frequent pinning.

The Dinner Hour, Wigan. Oil, signed and dated 1874 by Eyre Crowe, ARA (1824-1910). Exhibited at the Royal Academy 1874.
"It is a pity Mr. Crowe wasted his time on such unattractive materials" (*The Athenaeum*).

"Clogs and shawl" summed up the mill worker's life and dress.
Robert Roberts' book, *The Classic Slum,* describes Salford in the 1900's, and gives an anecdote of a girl who was sent to work in a weaving shed, as her family was in dire need of the extra wage. But she came from a suburb of houses with front parlours and little back gardens, and to be seen in clogs and shawl would put paid to the family's social aspirations. So she turned up at work in a coat and shoes, and sixty years later still recalled the "stares, sneers and skits" of the other girls, who considered her "a forward little bitch".

Roberts notes that weavers were at the top of the social and wage-earning scale, followed by winders and drawers-in. Spinners were paid less, and because of the slippery floors and the heat, they worked barefoot, dressed in "little more than calico shifts". This was considered less respectable and even morally a little questionable. Dye-workers had a dirty, heavy and wet job, and their neighbours regarded them accordingly.

Less distinctive dress began to oust "clogs and shawl" among the younger workers after the First World War, though older women could be seen wearing shawls in the streets of Manchester for many years after that.
Clogs are very sensible and comfortable footwear in many industries, and are still manufactured in the North of England. Special protective clogs and orthopaedic footwear are made, as well as fancy styles for dancing.
Individual makers may use special decorative motifs as a "trademark" on the uppers of dress clogs, though the regional variations in pattern have largely died out.

Bryant and May matchgirls, photographed in the 1860's wearing crinolines at work. Twenty years later in 1888, the match-girls' strike, under the championship of Annie Besant, became a landmark in British labour history.

The Second-hand Clothes Market

For the poor, the second-hand clothes trade provided an essential service, and though women could sew for themselves and their children, many had few leisure moments for needlework. Menswear could be bought cheap from "slop" tailoring establishments, but to buy good second-hand articles was often the best economy. As a London dealer told Henry Mayhew (*London Labour and the London Poor* 1851-62): "I'll back a coat such as is sometimes sold by a gentleman's servant to wear out two new slops".

Dealers wasted little, and were shrewd judges of the market.
Men's greatcoats, pilot coats and frock coats were the best sellers in the London markets of Petticoat Lane and Rosemary Lane. Working men had no need of dress coats, and "The clerks and shopmen are often tempted by the price, I was told, to buy some wretched new slop thing rather than a superior coat second-hand. The dress coats, however, are used for caps.
Sometimes a coat, for which the collector may have given 9d, is cut up for the repair of better garments".

Trousers were a very fast selling line, from smart ones to tough corduroys sold to Irish bricklayers. It is interesting to note that trousers, particularly the informal styles, are probably the single most difficult item of costume for museums to collect. Waistcoats with worn edges to the fronts had the frayed parts cut away, and could be remade as waistcoats, a size or two smaller. Velvet and satin waistcoats were re-sold for best wear. Cloth from waistcoats and other menswear might serve as the legs of women's cloth-topped boots.

Second-hand clothes dealers at Moses-square, Houndsditch *Illustrated Times* January 11th, 1862.

Woollens of all sorts, if they could no longer serve as garments, would be parcelled up for re-cycling. Cloth rags were ground down, mixed with new wool, and re-spun as shoddy. Dewsbury, Yorkshire, was the centre of the shoddy trade, and dusty and dirty work it was. Shoddy cloth was used for cheap mass clothing, service uniforms for the ranks, for blankets, drugget and table covers. Waste dust from the shoddy mills was used as manure on the hop-fields of Kent. This explains the legend on the tailboard of a Yorkshire lorry which amused a recent *Guardian* letter-writer: "Another Quality Load from X's Shoddy Manures".

Old boots and shoes could be "translated" by blacking and patches, and even by tricks with brown paper, to produce new-looking footwear. It seems that city labourers were more inclined than countrymen to wear second-hand shoes. Agricultural workers took a pride in strong new boots; an essential, though considerable, expense.

The Old Clothes Fair Camp Field, Manchester, water colour by Frederick Shields (1833-1911). A version painted in 1874 of his picture published in *The Graphic* of December 17th 1870. (Manchester City Art Gallery).

Women's clothing was less subject to change and translation, for the purchasers themselves had the skill to carry out alterations.
Old woollen and cotton gowns might be cut up for children's wear.
A silk dress in good condition could be cleaned up, and would sell, but shabby silks presented a problem to the dealer. They might be cut up as lining material for clothes or for work-boxes and dressing-cases; they might make children's spencers and bonnets, or be used for doll's clothes. But whereas wool and cotton could be shoddied, and linen rags went to the paper mills, silk rags had no value as salvage.

Cotton gowns, like the ones the factory girls are trying on in Frederick Shields picture *The Old Clothes Market, Camp Field,* would come up fresh when taken home and laundered, and they sold well. Woollen stuff dresses were less easy to smarten up, and were not so popular.

Cotton print gowns, by the 1860's, were associated chiefly with servants and working class women, and were not much worn by the fashionable middle classes. This is reflected in museum collections, where print morning gowns are common from the 1820's and '30's, while after about 1840 silks and satins predominate.

Henry Mayhew's informants gave him an interesting sidelight on the second hand fur trade. London prostitutes liked furs not just as finery, but as protection from the night air, and a dealer "could readily sell any 'tidy' article, tippet, boa, or muff, to those females, if they had from 2s. 6d. to 5s. at command". Maidservants liked a fur tippet, if they could afford it, for running errands in bad weather. Children's furs sold well, but working class women did not wear muffs.

139

The Old Clothes Market   Camp Field, Manchester

"The old clothes market" or "Rag Fair" as it is sometimes called, which is held every Monday and Saturday on Camp Field, in Manchester, is a singularly interesting scene, crowded with curious features, which strikingly illustrate the humblest phases of industrial life in that great Northern city. In dress, manners and speech, the people who frequent that "Rag Fair" are unlike any gatherings of the kind to be met with in any part of the kingdom. There may be a peculiar touch of dinginess, and even of pallor, about them, arising from their place and way of life, but they are none the less interesting on that account . . .

"The Old Clothes Market" where thread-bare garments, translated by the cunning hand of the cleaner and mender into a delusive freshness, are sold to the needy poor of the busy city.

. . . As we enter the first part of the open market ground . . . our eyes are caught by a tall Irishman, standing upon a wooden stage, which is piled with old clothes. His wife is by his side, handing the goods to him for sale. She is a strong-looking woman, with high cheek-bones, and a powerful jaw, and she has a very red nose, slightly damaged in the bridge. Her husband is a tall raw-boned man, with a sad countenance, but his eyes are bright, and there is no mistake about his nationality. ". . . look at thim trousers!" cries he, "Look at thim trousers! Divil a hair worse they are than the day they were made! Will e'er a one of yers gi' me a bid? Bad cess to me, but ye're a hard lot to dale with! Here,—I'll say, three-an'-three for 'em! Here,—three shillin'. Holy waiver now, won't ye give a man a chance! Here,—two-an-nine!" (giving the trousers a slap with his hand) "Two-an-nine. I'll ax no more and I'll take no less—take 'em or leave 'em. Sold agin!" cries he, spitting upon the money in his hand. "Sold agin,—to a gentleman worth a thousand a-year!" . . . The greatest part of the ground about is covered in patches, with old hats, old boots, and shoes, and other cast-off articles of apparel—each with its owners by its side on the look-out for custom . . . And, as we wander about among these outspread piles of clothing, many an interesting sight meets the eye. Here, a pale, poorly-clad woman is cheapening a pair of worn trousers for her husband at home, and she has the key of her cottage hung upon her little finger. There a poor mother is bargaining for a waistcoat for her little lad, whose only clothing is a bit of thin shirt and a pair of tattered trousers, slung by one brace. She is trying to get the waistcoat for fourpence. She succeeds at last, and away they go, the little fellow marching before, "donned" in his new waistcoat "as pert as a magpie". Yonder a factory girl has come to buy a dress. Her friend is holding her dress up to her, to see how it will fit. She says that it is rather too long-waisted, and "it'll want takkin' in a bit; but w' very little awlteration it'll do very weel . . ." Here a grey-haired man, with spectacles on nose, is poring over a newspaper till a customer comes; there, a mother has brought her children with her to the market, and they are tumbling about, half-naked, among the clothing; there, another is suckling her infant whilst she haggles with a customer about the price of an old coat; and yonder, a jolly looking fellow sits smoking, with a pot of ale peeping out under his stool. There is no end to such pictures on this spot. But the features of human character in this Old Clothes Market are far too rich and varied for the space at our command."

The Graphic December 17th 1870. Vol. II. No. 55

Engraving from *The Graphic* December 17th 1870 of Frederick Shields' picture *The Old Clothes Fair* Camp Field, Manchester.

The rag trade, whether first or second hand, has been a haven for immigrant peoples, since it requires the minimum of tools and equipment. Even the poorest and most frightened of refugees can carry their skills across national boundaries. At one time the second hand trade was dominated by Jewish families, but by the 1850's, when Mayhew was researching, the greater number of the dealers were Irish, driven out by the great potato famine of the late 1840's. The woman dealer in Shields' *Old Clothes Market* is unmistakably an Irishwoman, depicted in the idiom of Punch cartoons and illustrations in the popular papers. Accounts of rag fairs often dwell, in a manner which present day readers would perhaps find offensive, on the Jewish and Irish accents of the traders.

Markets have a picturesque appeal, with their bustle, patter, their tricks and dodges, and their slices of life and character. The rag fairs seem to have been an area of "low life" much enjoyed by journalists and graphic artists of the nineteenth century. Every major city had its old clothes market. The success of the trade, and its abhorrence of waste, is borne out in museum collections today. No wonder little working dress survives.

The Seaside

Souvenir Card by Kershaw and
Co. London c. 1860-65

Since the 18th century, seaside towns had been frequented by those anxious to benefit from the medicinal properties of sea water and fresh air. Like the inland spa-towns, they gradually became fashionable meeting places with their own high society. Brighton especially flourished, under the patronage of the Prince Regent.

With the age of steam boats and railways, their elegance was invaded by a new clientele. Aristocratic visitors now had to brush shoulders with day-trippers and weekly holiday makers—usually well heeled and middle class, but sometimes "persons of a lower order". It seemed as if the whole country had no other aspiration than to spend summer beside the seaside. Thousands descended on Scarborough, Margate or Llandudno, and in their wake came Punch and Judy men, musicians, acrobats, ice-cream vendors, street photographers and every other type of tradesman anxious for a quick profit. By the 1850s, the traditional British seaside had arrived, with its beach donkeys, piers and boarding houses with sea views and fat landladies.

The summer holiday was one aspect of the general growth of leisure activities which occurred in the middle of the century. This change in the pattern of many people's lives was reflected in their clothing. At the seaside, many of the town's social taboos could be forgotten. The stiff etiquette of formal dress gave way to happy clothes designed for fun and games.

The would-be holidaymaker was advised in *Manners of Modern Society* (1872) that:
> "a costume for picnics, excursions, and for seaside wear should be of a useful character. Nothing looks worse at these times than a thin, flimsy fabric, which will split and tear at every turn, or a faded shabby silk; and nothing looks better than some strong material either one that will wash, or otherwise, but of such a description that it will look almost as well at the end of a day's hard wear as at the beginning . . . Yachting dresses are generally made of serge or tweed, as being unspoilable by sea-air and water, and at the same time possessing warmth and durability." For men,
> "for seaside and country use, a complete suit of grey tweed is found the most suitable wear."

Warner's Etiquette for Gentlemen (1866) described the gentleman's "morning dress of the seaside" as "light coats, wideawake hats, caps, or straw hats".

Miss Barepole in the late Gale,
With topsails carried away.

SCENE ON THE SANDS.
Master Tommy won't go in the sea.

Poor Phipps in a Pretty Predicament.
Lost his Clothes bathing on the Sands, and
obliged to borrow anything he can get.

MOONLIGHT ON THE SANDS.
CHARMING EFFECT

Souvenir Cards by J. S. and Co. London c.1860-65

White corded cotton two piece
dress trimmed with black braid
1865-70
Split straw hat trimmed with
black petersham ribbon 1867-70

Washable dresses in bright prints were favourites for holiday wear. They
lasted for years, and examples in Platt Hall remain fresh and attractive
looking today. Some were made in crisp white piqué, with intricate
decorations stitched on in black braid, forming a striking contrast. A loose
jacket and good serge walking skirt were indispensable for more vigorous
activities. In 1860, the skirt would be rather short, perhaps looped up to show
broderie anglaise petticoats, striped cotton stockings and Balmoral boots with
broguing and little heels. This ensemble could be worn with a crinoline,
which would dance and swing in the sea breeze, much to the delight of
gentlemen with telescopes and the manufacturers of the rude postcards which
were beginning to make their appearance. The dramatic change in female
headgear in the 1850s may have been partly precipitated by seaside fashions.
At first, daring young women took to wearing wide brimmed Amazon hats
and small pillboxes instead of the all enclosing bonnet (which by the sea had
often been worn with an "ugly"—a kind of cane and fabric sun-screen which
came over the face). By the 1860s these were "de rigeur" not only on holiday
but also for everyday use.

Left: Cream wool suit printed with red and mauve flowers and Paisley type border pattern 1860-62
Cream felt hat with mauve velvet and feather 1860-65.

Below: Two straw hats 1855-65 and milliner's dummy head in papier mâché and plaster of paris 1840-60

Left: White muslin dress printed with blue
anemones 1862-7
Chinese style hat in straw trimmed with blue
velvet 1865-70
Right: White checked gauze dress printed with
mauve chrysanthemums 1862-4
White horsehair braid bonnet trimmed mauve
ribbons and violets 1865-7

Top: White muslin printed with broad stripes of shawl type pattern in reds and mauves.
Waist sash edged with frayed green silk 1860-65
Hat—plaited straw trimmed with black machine lace, artificial wild roses, daisies and ferns 1865-75. Black elastic loop. Label "Osborn's West End Emporium for hats and bonnets . . . 55-65 Edgware Road."

Below: white cotton with large check weave, trimmed with emerald green satin ribbon 1866-8. Pale green silk crêpe hat with pale green silk base, mauve artificial flowers and black elastic loop 1865-70.

RYDE PIER.

Ryde

The first view of Ryde from the water, to the verge of which trees grow thickly, is very striking. Ryde is divided into Upper and Lower, the former being the older town, called anciently Rye . . . The streets are open and pleasant, the best being "The Terrace", from which fine views are commanded. Houses and villas are springing up in every direction, and Ryde promises to become by far the largest town in the Isle of Wight. The pier, extending seaward for about half a mile, was opened in 1814, but has since been considerably lengthened. It forms an excellent promenade, and is well supplied with seats, some of which are covered. From the pier extends the esplanade, a long drive over part of the beach, formerly called the Duver, where many of the crew of the "Royal George", whose bodies came ashore here, were buried.

Ventnor

. . . All the beautiful scenery of the Undercliff is easily accessible from Ventnor, which itself occupies a very picturesque part of it. . . . At Ventnor there are (or were) some bold vertical sections of the firstone; and an enormous mass of rock overhangs the road east of the Marine Parade. The vicinity is rich in the shells and zoophytes of the cretaceous system; and chalkmarl fossils abound at the Shute above Ventnor.

Illustrated London News 1859. vol 35. p.256.

"Wish You Were Here!"
Cartes de visite c.1865.
Top left: By A. Grant, Kirkcaldy.
Top middle: Shanklin, Isle of Wight
by the Surrey Photographic Co.
Guildford.
Top right: St. Lawrence
Church, Isle of Wight, by
Knight and Sons, Ventnor.
Below left: "Anstey's Cove near
Torquay".
Below right: By Symonds and
Wheeler, West Cowes, Isle of
Wight.

Souvenir card by Kershaw and
Son, London. Number 1166.
1850s.

"Now don't I look a pretty figure?"

Another seaside garment, or rather its absence, was the subject of much
discussion. When men wanted to bathe, they simply took all their clothes off
and ran into the water. This was usual in public as well as private spots and
caused much embarrassment. In the 1860s, W. F. Taylor published a
pamphlet on sea-bathing, in which he stated "Everyone has been at some
watering place—and it is not necessary therefore, for me to enter into very
elaborate particulars. Were it so, my pen would have to be laid down, for the
scenes which are daily complained of . . . are practically indescribable in print
. . . there are rows of houses along the beach from which without the aid of an
opera glass the bathing operations are clearly visible—some houses from
which the bathers may be very easily recognised, and some from which it is
unsafe for a lady to look at bathing time, lest her delicacy should be outraged."
(*Suitable Bathing Dresses as used in Biarritz with Instructions on
Swimming.*)

Taylor was advocating a loose, two-piece bathing suit for both sexes, similar to
those worn on the continent, so that ladies and gentlemen could stroll along
the beach together and swim with complete propriety.
In England, small swimming trunks were beginning to be used—especially
supplied by the owners of bathing machines—those huts on wheels in which
the person changed, were conveyed to the water's edge, and sometimes
screened from public view by a canopy as they climbed down the steps
into the water.

In his diary, the Rev. Francis Kilvert described an encounter with these
novelties in 1873.
"At Seaton, while Dora was sitting on the beach, I had a bathe.
A boy brought me to the machine door, two towels as I thought, but when I
came out of the water and began to use them I found that one of the rags he
had given me was a pair of very short red and white striped drawers to cover
my nakedness. Unaccustomed to such things and customs, I had in my
ignorance bathed naked and set at naught the conventionality of the place
and scandalized the beach. However, some little boys who were looking at
the rude naked man appeared to be much interested in the spectacle, and
the young ladies who were strolling near seemed to have no objection".

Opposite and below: Brown alpaca female bathing suit, trimmed with red woollen braid 1865-75. Brown silk bathing hat printed with blue circles with white dots, and bound with blue silk. Blue silk ribbons with woven floral pattern c.1870. Bathing espadrilles with rope soles, beige cotton uppers, purple embroidery and tapes in wool, embroidered and painted portrait on the front of woman in French national costume c.1865-75.

Female bathing was always a much more private affair than male. The main problem with female bathing dress lay not in its deficiency but in its excess, which as Mr. Taylor considered, prevented anything more demanding than a timid dip from the steps of the bathing machine.

"The female Briton when bathing has a slight advantage over the male as far as civilized notions of propriety go, in as much as she generally wears a chemise or shirt of blue flannel, open at the chest and tied round the neck. It reaches a little below the knee, and is just long enough to make swimming impossible, but by no means adapted either in size or shape, to effectually answer the requirements of decency." This was in contrast to Biarritz, where "the ladies wear what may be described as a simple Bloomer costume, consisting of jackets, shaped variously according to taste, and loose trousers reaching to the ankle. The dress is completed by list slippers, to protect the feet from the shingle, and a straw hat, neatly trimmed, to protect the fair wearer's complexion."

We will never know if Mr. Taylor's campaign had any direct effect, but certainly by the end of the decade, ladies were wearing precisely the costume described, only substituting waterproof mobcaps for straw hats.

Augustus Leopold Egg 1816-63. *A Walk on the Beach* c.1855-60. Oil on Panel 35.5cm x 24.5cm unsigned.

Below: Croquet player c.1865 taken by J. Wilson, Liverpool.

Left: White twilled wool and cotton mixture skirt with woven black stripes, appliqué black velvet and coloured braids c.1870. Red wool "Garibaldi" blouse with black beads and white embroidery and black buttons c.1865-70. Black velvet hat with red and white feathers 1860-70.

"At a Party" *Cassell's Magazine*
New Series Vol IV p.401.
c.1873

Social Events in the 1870s

Tissot's *Hush!* 1875

Balls, dinners and private concerts such as the one depicted in Tissot's *Hush*! were high spots of Victorian social life. At these glittering occasions participants reaffirmed their position within the social élite through sumptuous dress and sparkling behaviour. There old friendships could be strengthened and new ones made. Christopher Wood wrote of this painting in *Victorian Panorama:*

> "Many attempts have been made to identify the party and the figures—the party is said to have been given by the Coops and the violinist has been variously identified as Madame Neruda, Diaz de Soria and Mlle. Castellan; other people identifiable include Lord Leighton, Prince Dhuleep Singh, Arthur Sullivan, and in the doorway two of Tissot's friends, Ferdinand Heilbuth and Giuseppe de Nittis . . . (Tissot) was the perfect society painter, because he painted society as it saw itself. Everyone looks distinguished, elegant and witty; even the rooms themselves are suffused with white, brilliant light from the chandeliers . . . Above all, Tissot was a painter of women. He was obsessed by pretty, elegant women, and perhaps no one has painted them with such devotion. Every inch of his women's dresses is delineated with extraordinary fidelity, at a time when female dress was at its most elaborate, expensive and beautiful."

This age saw the dawning of Haute Couture. Such women would have flocked to Paris to purchase their gowns, perhaps from that first and greatest of couturiers, Charles Worth. Each ensemble may have cost hundreds of pounds and been the product of hours of labour, yet none was designed to last through more than one or two such evenings. It seems incredible that so many frothy layers of fine tulle and silk flowers were intended to be sat on and crushed as they are by Tissot's models. The stiff fine gauze, the texture of which is so beautifully depicted in the hem of the black dress, snagged and ripped at the slightest touch. One damp journey home and its pristine freshness would have been transformed into a limp rag. These dresses expressed the wealth of their wearers, or rather that of the people who paid for them. Like fireworks, or banks of fresh flowers, they were brilliant statements of conspicuous consumption.

Opposite page:
Top: James Tissot *Hush*! exhibited 1875. Oil on canvas 73.7 x 112.9 cms. signed.
Bottom: Fan, with painted white satin leaf, ivory sticks and guards 1870-80. Length of stick 10¾".

153

154

This page:
Top right: Left figure: fawn satin trimmed with Brussels lace 1870-73. Label inside waistband: *Madame Devy's Company Ltd. 16 Grafton Street, Bond Street* (see Chapter 5 on Dressmaking).
Right figure: White cotton net over cream satin 1870-72.
Top left: Woman in evening dress by W. C. D. Donney, Newcastle Upon Tyne.
Above: Woman in evening dress by Heinr. Graf, Berlin. Both 1870-75.

Opposite page:
Top left: Pale blue satin dress trimmed black machine lace. Label on waistband *Howell, James and Co. 5, 7, 9, Regent Street, London.* 1871-3.
Right centre and below: Pale blue corded silk dress, trimmed pink corded silk, with cream lace. This has alternative day and evening bodices. Maker's label now illegible except *Newcastle upon Tyne.* 1871-3.
Below left: Fan with painted and gilt paper leaf, ivory sticks and guards. Mirror on one guard. 1860-70.

These dresses were intended to be cast aside and the few which survive today are often shadows of their former glory. With their tatty ribbons and flowers and grubby sad frills, they would not have looked out of place in Miss Havisham's boudoir! When worn, they would have conveyed an impression of fresh, carefree innocence, in keeping with the conventional ideals of young womanhood. The stately matron was expected to wear rich heavy fabrics, such as satin and velvet, to demonstrate her seniority as a married woman and to indicate that, provided with a husband and his money, she was (theoretically) no longer interested in love games. In contrast, the young girl's costume signalled her availability. Rich fabrics and jewels were considered as improper on her as maidenly fripperies on the mature form. Anyone past their late twenties who did not dress suitably to their age risked being called "mutton dressed as lamb".

Such costumes reflect the social status of their wearers in another way, through their power to shock. The dresses of the upper and middle classes revealed more and more of the female body and comments were continually made on the subject. An anecdote is told of Bishop Monk: at a party, a lady in a décolleté gown excited a good deal of attention. Someone remarked to the bishop "Her appearance is really quite scandalous. Did you ever see anything like it?" "Never", replied the bishop, "at least, not since I was weaned!" (*Leaves from the notebooks of Lady Dorothy Neville.* Ed Ralph Neville 1907).

Ordinary working people would never have dreamed of wearing low cut dresses; this would have been quite immoral and their wearers, if of their own class, were considered "shameless hussies". An interesting example of this attitude is given in Trollope's *Barchester Towers.* When Miss Thorne held a large afternoon fête, the local gentry and well-to-do townspeople were invited into the house for refreshments, while the estate workers and yeoman farmers were entertained in a marquee outside. The Lookalofts, a humble farming family with visions of grandeur, presented themselves indoors with the gentry, the daughters wearing inappropriate and extremely low cut dresses. This incident was related to their neighbours, who condemned their costume.

Above: "Ada Gillis" by the New School of Photography, 29 Euston Road. c.1870.
Below: Stereoscopic photograph of preparations for a ball. Pinpricks through the paper create bright points of light at candles and lamp c.1865.
Opposite: Fashion Plate from the *English Woman's Domestic Magazine* Vol XX 1876.

"Mrs. Greenacre exclaimed, 'And she told you them people was up there in the drawing room?'.
'She told me she zeed them come in—that they was dressed finer by half nor any of the family, with all their neckses and buzoms stark naked as a born babby'.
'The Minxes!' exclaimed Mrs. Greenacre, who felt herself more put about by this than any other mark of aristocratic distinction which her enemies had assumed.
'Yes, indeed' continued Mrs. Guffern, 'as naked as you please, while all the quality was dressed just as you and I be, Mrs. Greenacre'."

Imp. H^{tte} Lefevre, Paris

Ad. Goubaud & Fils, Ed^{rs} Paris

127

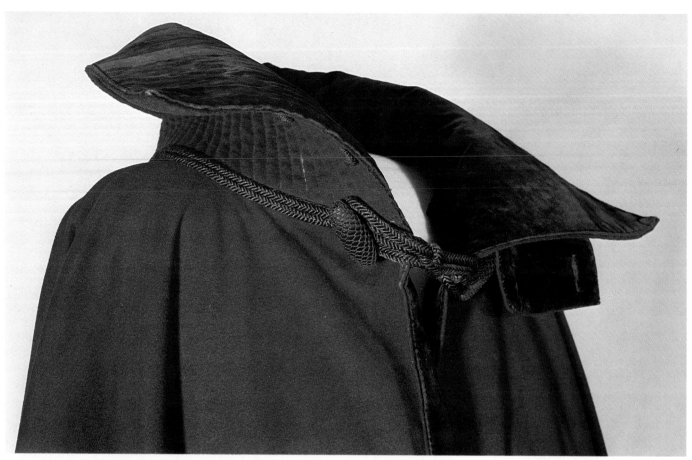

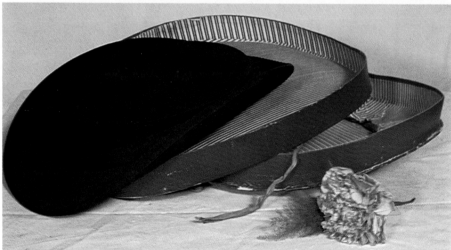

Top and right: Navy blue cloth evening cloak with velvet collar. Mid 19th century. Belonged to Colonel Oliver Ormerod Walker of Chesham, Lancashire 1833-1914 or his father of the same name.

Above and centre: Mid-19th century collapsible top hat of the type known as a "Gibus" after its inventor who perfected it in 1840. Cream twilled silk neckcloth with woven floral pattern probably made at Walker's Mill, Salford. 1840-70.

Male dress for social events was as simple as female dress was grand.
An etiquette book from around 1880 at Platt Hall states "a black tail-coat,
waistcoat and trousers, and white tie, although presenting a sombre
appearance, are the proper wear, and, unless where eccentricity is apparent,
prevail at the dinner table and at evening parties (two items in this costume
which admit of discretion among "men who dress" viz, the vest and tie,
both of which may be either white or black, without any infraction of the
laws of "bienseance". This, however, must be settled by the taste of the
wearer, who should remember that black having the effect of diminishing a
man's size, and white that of increasing it, it would, therefore, be judicious
for a person of unusual size to tone down his extra bulk by favouring black
in both these articles . . . we, however must confess a decided partiality for
a white necktie, at least; because although subject to the disadvantage of
being "de rigeur" amongst waiters, it is nevertheless always considered
unexceptional at any season or hour, in any rank, profession, or capacity . . .

For appendages, eschew all flash stones: nothing is more unexceptionable
for sleeve-buttons and the fastenings of the front of the shirt than fine gold,
fashioned in some simple form, sufficiently massive to indicate use and
durability, and skillfully and handsomely wrought, if
ornamented at all . . . As regards gloves, a fresh
white, or what amounts at night to the same
thing, a pale yellow glove is the only admissible
thing for balls, other evening parties,
ceremonious dinners, and wedding receptions."
Complete Etiquette for Gentlemen, c.1880.
Another etiquette book from the previous
generation advised:
"Gloves are indispensably
necessary in a ballroom.
It would be quite as correct
for a gentleman to be seen
dancing without his coat
as without his gloves.
When taking refreshment
pull them off; it is as
vulgar to eat in gloves as
it is to dance without
them."
*Etiquette for Ladies and
Gentlemen,* c.1850.

Fashion Plate from the *West End Gazette,* January 1873.
This has been used by a customer to order a suit;
note the inked in alteration to the right figure's tails.

Reading List

General Introductions to Studying Costume
Valerie Cumming
Exploring Costume History 1500-1900
Batsford 1982

Janet Arnold
A Handbook of Costume
Macmillan 1973

General Costume History and Theory
Janet Arnold
Patterns of Fashion Vol I 1660-1860
                 Vol II 1860-1940
Wace 1966

Quentin Bell
On Human Finery
Hogarth Press 2nd ed. 1976

Nancy Bradfield
Costume in Detail: Women's Dress 1730-1930
Harrap 1968

Anne Buck
Victorian Costume and Costume Accessories
Herbert Jenkins 1961

Anne Buck
Dress in Eighteenth Century England
Batsford 1979

Penny Byrde
The Male Image—
   Men's Fashion in England 1300-1970
Batsford 1979

C. Willett Cunnington
Feminine Attitudes in the Nineteenth Century
Heinemann 1935

C. Willett Cunnington
The Art of English Costume
Collins 1948

C. W. Cunnington
English Women's Clothing in the 19th Century
Faber & Faber 1937

C. W. Cunnington
English Women's Clothing in the Present Century
Faber & Faber 1952

C. W. & P. Cunnington
Handbook of Medieval Costume
Handbook of English Costume in the 16th Century
Handbook of English Costume in the 17th Century
Handbook of English Costume in the 18th Century
Handbook of English Costume in the 19th Century
Handbook of English Costume in the 20th Century
Faber & Faber 1954-59

Millia Davenport
The Book of Costume
Crown Publishers, New York 1st ed. 1948

Alison Gernsheim
Fashion and Reality 1840-1914
Faber & Faber 1964

Doris Langley Moore
Fashion Through Fashion Plates 1771-1970
Ward Lock 1971

James Laver
Taste and Fashion
Harrap 1937 (new eds.)

James Laver
A Concise History of Costume
Thames and Hudson 1969

The Gallery of English Costume, Manchester
Picture Book No. 1. Women's Costume 'A Brief View'
Picture Book No. 2. Women's Costume 18th century
Picture Book No. 3. Women's Costume 1800-1835
Picture Book No. 4. Women's Costume 1835-1870
Picture Book No. 5. Women's Costume 1870-1900
Picture Book No. 6. Women's Costume 1900-1930
Picture Book No. 7. Children's Costume 1800-1900
Picture Book No. 8. Women's Costume for Sport
Picture Book No. 9. Fashion in Miniature (Dolls)
Picture Book No. 10. Weddings 1735-1970

Geoffrey Squire
Dress Art and Society 1560-1970
Studio Vista 1974

Norah Waugh
The Cut of Men's Clothes 1600-1900
Faber & Faber 1964

The Cut of Women's Clothes 1600-1930
Faber & Faber 1968

Background Sources
The Connoisseur Period Guides
—ed. Ralph Edwards & L.G.G. Ramsey
The Late Georgian Period 1760-1810
The Regency Period 1810-1830
The Early Victorian Period 1830-1860
The Connoisseur 1958

Mark Girouard
Life in the English Country House
Penguin 1978

William Royle
Rusholme: Past and Present—
   Being a Gossipy Talk of Men and Things
Wm. Hough & Sons, 2 Swan Court,
Manchester 1905

Christopher Wood
Victorian Panorama—Paintings in Victorian Life
Faber & Faber 1976

Special Subjects: Textiles
John Irwin and Katharine B. Brett
Origins of Chintz
H.M.S.O. 1970

Florence M. Montgomery
Printed Textiles. English and American Cottons
   and Linens 1700-1850
Thames and Hudson 1970

Deryn O'Connor and Hero Granger-Taylor
Colour and the Calico Printer
An Exhibition of Printed
and Dyed Textiles 1750-1850 (Catalogue)
West Surrey College of Art & Design 1982

Stuart Robinson
A History of Printed Textiles
Studio Vista 1969

V & A Museum
English Printed Textiles 1720-1836
H.M.S.O. 1960

Special Subjects
Alison Adburgham
Shops and Shopping
George Allen and Unwin 1964

Ruth Brandon
A Capitalist Romance
   —Singer and the Sewing Machine
J. B. Lippincott & Co. 1977

Penelope Byrde
A Frivolous Distinction
Fashion and Needlework in the Works of Jane Austen
Bath City Council 1979

Duncan Bythell
The Sweated Trades—
    Outwork in Nineteenth Century Britain
Batsford 1978

C. W. Cunnington
Looking Over My Shoulder
Faber & Faber 1961

Phillis Cunnington and Alan Mansfield
English Costume for Sports and Outdoor Recreation
A. & C. Black 1969

Phillis Cunnington and Catherine Lucas
Costume for Births, Marriages and Deaths
A. & C. Black 1972

Phillis Cunnington
Costume of Household Servants
A. & C. Black 1974

Phillis Cunnington and Catherine Lucas
Charity Costumes
A. & C. Black 1978

C. W. & P. Cunnington ed. Valerie Mansfield
The History of Underclothes
Faber & Faber 2nd edit. 1981

Madeleine Ginsburg
Wedding Dress 1740-1970
H.M.S.O. 1981

Michael Hiley
Victorian Working Women: Portraits from Life
Gordon Fraser 1979

James Laver
Dandies
Weidenfeld and Nicolson 1968

Ann Monsarrat
And the Bride Wore . . .
The story of the white wedding
Gentry Books 1973

Christina Walkley and Vanda Foster
Crinolines and Crimping Irons
Victorian Clothes;
How they were cleaned and cared for
Peter Owen 1978

Christina Walkley
The Ghost in the Looking Glass—
    The Victorian Seamstress
Peter Owen 1981

Primary Sources (All are included in the
Platt Hall Costume Library except those marked*)

The Art of Dress or Guide to the Toilette
Charles Tilt 1839

*Samuel Bamford
The Autobiography of Samuel Bamford 1788-1872
Frank Cass & Co. 1967

The Book of English Trades and Library
of Useful Arts
Printed for Sir Richard Phillips & Co.
12th Edition 1824

*Frederick Engels
The Condition of the Working Class in England
Granada 1982 (1845)

Etiquette for Ladies and Gentlemen or
The Principles of True Politeness
Milner & Co. c.1850

*Etiquette for Gentlemen
Warner's 1866

*Manners of Modern Society—Being a Book of
Etiquette
Cassell, Petter & Galpin 1872

Complete Etiquette for Gentlemen
Ward Lock c.1880

Thomas Hearn
Rudiments of Cutting Coats etc. of all sizes to fit
the human form by anatomical proportions in
conjunction with geometrical principles
Printed and sold by the Author 1819

J. W. Hayes
The Draper and Haberdasher
Houlston's Industrial Library 1878

Derek Hudson
Munby: Man of Two Worlds
Abacus 1974

*Anne Hughes
The Diary of a Farmer's Wife 1796-7
Penguin 1981

*Rev. Francis Kilvert
Kilvert's Diary: Selections from the diary of the
Reverend Francis Kilvert 1870-79
ed. William Plomer
Book Club Associates 1944

The Ladies' Own Memorandum Book 1774

A Lady
The Lady's Economical Assistant
1808

A Lady
The Sampler, or a System of
Teaching Needlework in Schools
G. C. Caines 1850

The Manual of Needlework for the
Use of National Schools
Commissioners of National Education, Ireland 1873

Henry Mayhew
London Labour and the London Poor
Frank Cass & Co. 1967 (1st Ed. 1851-1862)

Mrs. Merrifield
Dress as a Fine Art
Arthur Hall, Virtue & Co. 1854

Elias Moses & Son
Handbooks c.1840-c.1860
e.g. The Record of Public Sentiments 1855
        The Commercial Cornucopia 1855
        The Pillars of Trade 1856

Neckclothitania or Tietania being an Essay on
Starchers by one of the Cloth
J. J. Stockdale (pub.) 1818

*Lady Dorothy Neville
Reminiscences Ed. Ralph Neville
Thomas Nelson & Sons 1906

*Leaves from the Notebooks of Lady Dorothy Neville.
Ed. Ralph Neville
Macmillan & Co. 1907

E. E. Perkins
The Lady's Shopping Manual and Mercery Album
Thomas Hurst 1834
then called Treatise on Haberdashery and
Hosiery in editions until 1870s

Robert Roberts
The Classic Slum
Salford Life in the First quarter of the Century
Pelican 1971

Diana Sperling
Mrs Hurst Dancing
Victor Gollancz Ltd 1981

Albert Smith
The National History of the Gent
David Bogue 1847

Albert Smith
The Flirt
Ward Lock & Co. 1848

Ed. Albert Smith
Gavarni in London: Sketches of Life and Character
David Bogue 1849

*W. F. Taylor
Suitable Bathing Dresses as used in Biarritz
with Instructions on Swimming
Hamilton & Co. c.1860

Flora Thompson
Lark Rise to Candleford
Penguin Modern Classics 1945

The Useful Arts and Manufactures of Great Britain
Society for Promoting Christian Knowledge c.1845

George Walker
The Costume of Yorkshire
Caliban Books 1978 (1st Ed. 1814)

*James Woodforde
Diary of a Country Parson 1758-1802
Oxford University Press 1931

The Workwoman's Guide
Simpkin Marshall & Co. 1838

The Young Woman's Companion
1841

See also Works by
Jane Austen, Charles Dickens, George Eliot,
Elizabeth Gaskell, Richard Brinsley Sheridan,
Anthony Trollope

Select Periodicals (in Chronological Order)
(in Platt Hall Library)

The Ladies' Magazine	1770-1832
La Belle Assembleé	1806-1832
The World of Fashion	1824-1851
The Illustrated London News	1842-
The Ladies' Cabinet	1832-1870
Punch	1841-
The Journal of Design	1849-1852
The English Woman's Domestic Magazine	1852-1879
The Graphic	1870-

ACKNOWLEDGEMENTS
We wish to thank the Master and Fellows of Trinity
College, Cambridge, for permission to quote from
the diaries of Arthur Munby.
All the items illustrated, with the exception of the
doll on page 126, are in the collections of
Manchester City Art Galleries and the Gallery of
English Costume.